Curso Completo de Inglés

Teach Yourself

ENGLISH

Habla Inglés desde la primera lección.
Nivel Tres avanzado.
Aprenda Inglés sin profesor hoy.

Dr. Yeral E. Ogando

Curso Completo de Inglés – Nivel Tres
© 2016 por Dr. Yeral E. Ogando
Publicado: Christian Translation LLC
Impreso en los EE.UU
Diseño de Portada por SAL media

ISBN 13: 978-1-946249-00-5
ISBN 10: 1-946249-00-9

1. Language Learning - Aprender un Idioma.
2. English Language – Idioma Inglés

DEDICACIÓN:

Éste libro está dedicado a la Única y duradera persona que siempre ha estado ahí para mí, sin importar cuán terco soy:
DIOS

Sin Ti mi Dios, nada soy. Gracias por tu misericordia e inmerecedora Gracia.

AGRADECIMIENTOS:

Gracias a Dios por permitir que mi sueño se hiciera realidad y por darme fuerzas cuando sentí ganas de renunciar.

De no haber sido por el apoyo que he recibido a lo largo del camino de parte de éstas increíbles y sorprendentes personas, no estaría donde estoy hoy.

Gracias a mi editora, Sharon A. Lavy y a los "Diseñadores de la Portada", SAL media por haber hecho un gran trabajo ayudándome con esta obra.

Elizabeth McAchren por su excelente colaboración e ideas durante la creación de este tercer libro de la serie. Coleman Clarke y Kathryn Ganime-Leech por su increíble trabajo en el audio.

Ésta ha sido una muy larga jornada para mi familia, pero la recompensa es digna. Gracias a mi padre, Héctor y a mis hijas, Yeiris y Tiffany por permanecer a mi lado a través de éste viaje. Saben que les amo.

God bless you all
Dios les bendiga

Dr. Yeral E. Ogando
www.aprendeis.com

Table of Contents

Introducción

He publicado este método para que puedan aprender inglés en forma rápida y eficaz.

Les pido que dediquen 20 minutos diríos al estudio del inglés sin interrupción, para que puedan concentrarse y digerir el contenido de esta obra. Uno de los desafíos más grande del aprendizaje es ser una persona Autodidacta, en otras palabras, que aprende por cuenta propia. Se requiere mucha disciplina y dedicación en el estudio para poder lograr un buen aprendizaje. Estudiar una hora completa cada día puede hacerlos sentirse aburridos o cansados rápidamente, esta es la razón por la que les recomiendo un mínimo de 20 minutos y un máximo de 40 minutos al día para mejor aprendizaje. De este modo podrán lograr mejores resultados.

Les deseo Buena suerte en este increíble viaje al mundo del aprendizaje del idioma inglés, y recuerden, *"Hablen sin vergüenza"*

Dr. Yeral E. Ogando
www.aprendeis.com

7

SÍMBOLOS Y ABREVIACIONES

Audio: Indica que se necesita el Audio MP3 para esta sección. No olviden que cada oración o palabra en inglés está disponible en audio MP3.

Dialogo: Indica dialogo o texto de lectura.

Gramática: Indica la gramática o explicación de la estructura del idioma

Ejercicios: Indica las secciones para ejercicios y prácticas.

Prólogo

Muchas personas creen que *"Aprender Inglés"* es una tarea muy difícil, de modo que se pasan la vida con el deseo de Aprender Inglés, pero nunca se deciden por el miedo o tabú que se les han inculcado, que el Inglés es muy difícil de aprender.

Estoy completamente de acuerdo con las personas que dicen que es difícil Aprender Inglés, puesto que nunca han tenido el método adecuado o la enseñanza correcta para aprenderlo. En otras palabras, siempre será difícil Aprender Inglés sino se tiene la herramienta adecuada.

No olviden que no todo el que enseña, sabe enseñar. Existen muchos profesores y muchos métodos para aprender, sin embargo, la mayoría de ellos no abordan la forma correcta para el aprendizaje del estudiante. Este método ya les ha demostrado en el segundo nivel, lo sencillo que es poder "hablar Inglés" en poco tiempo. Después de mas de 10 años de experiencia y vivenciando la forma rápida del aprendizaje de mis estudiantes, pongo en sus manos este tesoro.

Les he demostrado lo fácil que es aprender este idioma usando mi método. Ya ustedes están hablando inglés, ahora necesitan desarrollar sus habilidades y hablar más fluido. No tienen que esperar meses y años, como ya han visto, podrán ver lo rápido que avanzarán en su nivel de conversación.

Este curso es para enseñarles la forma correcta de Aprender Inglés, reconociendo los patrones y formas de hablar; aun podrán aprender un poco más de español en este increíble viaje.

Siempre recomiendo a mis alumnos que estudien unmínimo de 20 minutos y un máximo de 40 minutos al dia. Esto les permitirá aprovechar al máximo su aprendizaje y a la vez a mantener la mente activa en el idioma. No traten de estudiar varias horas un dia a la semana, porque se fatigarán y aburrirán, no llegando a sacarle provecho al aprendizaje. Es mejor un poco con calidad que mucho sin efectividad.

Recuerden que los sonidos y pronunciaciones deberán ser escuchados y aprendidos en el transcurso del curso, usando la herramienta del audio para cada sección.

PASOS PARA USAR ESTE LIBRO Y SACARLE EL MEJOR PROVECHO

Asegúrense de **DESCARGAR** el Audio del libro con las instrucciones encontradas en la página "**BONO GRATIS**" este método no tiene la pronunciación marcada o habla de la pronunciación, es **IMPERATIVO** descargar el audio para poder aprender la pronunciación correcta del inglés.

Ve a la página de "**BONO GRATIS**" y descarga el audio del libro.

Lee la conversación del libro, escuchando la pronunciación directamente del audio. Asegúrate de captar la pronunciación y practicarla.

Lee y aprende las nuevas palabras, frases y expresiones encontradas en la sección "*New Words*" y "*Phrases and Expressions*".

Ahora debes concentrarte en la gramática de la lección. Esta es la parte más importante y lo que te permitirá hablar correctamente. Presta mucha atención a cada explicación y en especial a la estructura de las palabras. Recuerda que necesitas el audio para las oraciones o ejemplos encontrados en todo el libro. Nunca pases a otra sección o lección sin antes dominar completamente la gramática.

Ahora necesitas regresar al inicio de la lección y escuchar una vez más las conversaciones hasta que puedas comprenderlas bien y asimilar la estructura.

Repasa las nuevas palabras, frases y expresiones

hasta que las aprendas bien y asegúrate de lograr la pronunciación como la del audio. El desafío más grande que tienes es dominar la pronunciación y pronunciar como la voz nativa del audio MP3. Es tiempo de realizar los ejercicios. Asegúrate de llenar y practicar cada ejercicio. Los mismos medirán tu comprensión de la gramática de la lección. Una vez llenes tus ejercicios, revísalos una y otra vez, y cuando ya estés seguro. Entonces, podrás ver las respuestas al final del libro, solo para comparar y asegurarte de que lo hiciste bien. No hagas trampa. Ya terminaste la lección. Felicidades. Ahora debes regresar al inicio de la lección una vez más y repasarla por completo, como si fuera la primera vez. Si viste que los conceptos expresados los entendiste bien y los manejaste a la perfección, es porque estás listo para pasar a la siguiente lección. De lo contrario, entonces, deberás seguir el repaso de la lección hasta que la domines a la perfección.

Lesson 1
I can't wait to graduate – No veo la hora de graduarme

Conversation

Mark: Hey, look at this. There are a bunch of high-paying jobs in the classified ads today. It says here they need a security guard, and they'll pay $24 an hour.

Steve: That's not bad.

Mark: No. Oh, but you have to have experience in public service.

Steve: Well, you know, my work as a fireman qualifies me for that. But I'd have to give two weeks' notice.

Mark: Yeah. And they need someone right now. Here's something different. They want someone to design video games.

Steve: Well, you can do that yourself.

Mark: No, I don't know anything about programming. I just know how to use design software. You're qualified for both of these jobs.

Steve: Are they full time?

Mark: Yeah. Oh, you're right. You wouldn't be able to finish your degree this year if you worked full time. Whatever you do, don't quit school.

Steve: Don't worry. I don't plan to. But I can't wait to graduate!

New words – Nuevas palabras

All over – por todos lados / en todas partes / por doquier

Altitude - altitud

Boot - bota

Camper - campista

Campground - campamento

Captain - capitán

Carpenter - carpintero

Cashier - cajero

Change - cambio

College - colegio / universidad

Computer programmer – programador de computadoras

Degree – grado *(refiriéndose a la temperatura, también en otro contexto significa título universitario)*

Electrician - electricista

Farmer – granjero / agricultor

Firefighter - bombero

Fisherman - pescador

Folks – gente / pueblo *(usado para personas que conoces o tu familia "mi gente")*

Fortune - fortuna

Heel – taco / tacón

Hit – éxito *(una canción se vuelve un hit)*

Indigestion - indigestión

Industry - industria

Joke – broma / chiste

Judge - juez

Kid – muchacho (a)

Lawyer - abogado
Liter - litro
Luck - suerte
Make-up - maquillaje
Oven - horno
Plumber - plomero
Razor (blade) – rasuradora
Recipe - receta
Repairman – reparador / técnico
Sailor – marino
Sale - venta
Sand - arena
Shoelace – cordón de zapato
Soldier - soldado
Souvenir - recuerdo
Speed - velocidad
Tent - tienda
Tour – gira / recorrido
Tour guide – guía turística
Tourism - turismo
Toys - juguetes
Tramp – vagabundo / pordiosero
Village - villa

Words Definitions

Keep in touch: *when we want to tell someone to write us or call us because we want to keep communication open.*

By the way: *When we want to change the conversation because we remember something.*

Likewise: *when we think or feel the same as the*

other person; a transition used to add another point.

Can't wait: *when we are happy because we want something to happen soon or we want to do it soon.*

Phrases and Expressions - Frases y expresiones
A bunch of – un montón de
Back home – pueblo natal / hogar *(se usa esta expresión para referirse al hogar o pueblo natal de uno, cuando no estamos ahí)*
By the way – a propósito
Classified ads – Anuncios clasificados
Don't quit school – no dejes (abandones) la escuela
High-paying jobs – trabajos bien pagos
To give two weeks' notice – dar dos semanas de pre-aviso (para dejar un trabajo)

Can't wait for (Can't wait to) – no veo el momento, no puedo esperar por, estoy deseando *(se usa esta expresión cuando estamos ansioso por que algo pase o acontezca. Usamos "can't wait to" cuando viene un verbo.* **Can't wait to see you** – *estoy loco por verte / anhelo verte)*
Come on – dime *(usamos esta expresión cuando queremos que nos digan lo que realmente paso. También Se usa para convencer a alguien que haga cualquier cosa. Vente conmigo. Trabaja el sábado. Dame tu postre. No le digas a mamá.)*
Darn – rayos *(usamos esta expresión cuando estamos enojados o cuando nos damos un golpe, los españoles dirían "joder", algunos latinos diríamos "coño")*

Nivel Tres

Dear – querido (a)

Howdy - ¿Cómo te va? *(es una expresión muy coloquial para decir, "que tal" usada en el norte de Texas)*

I thought she'd never leave – pensé que nunca se iría.

In the way – en medio / en el camino *(usamos esta expresión cuando alguien se mete en nuestro camino)*

It was nice talking to you – fue bueno hablar contigo

Keep in touch – mantente en contacto

Likewise – igualmente / de igual forma

On sale – en venta

Out of the way – fuera del camino *(usamos esta expresión cuando queremos que alguien se nos quite del medio, nos deje el camino libre, o para decir que no nos estorben)*

Take care - cuídate

To be called – ser llamado *(llamar a alguien, algo o algún lugar por su nombre)*

To go camping – irse de campamento

To go sailing – irse a navegar

To help yourself – ayudarse a uno mismo *(usualmente comiendo o bebiendo algo. También la usamos cuando le decimos a alguien "Help yourself" sírvete tú mismo o estás en tu casa)*

To look forward to – anhelar que algo suceda *(siempre va un verbo después de "to")*

To wish someone the best of luck – desearle a alguien buena suerte

Welcome - bienvenido
Welcome aboard – bienvenido a bordo
Who is it by? - ¿Quién canta? / ¿Quién lo escribió?
(usamos esta expresión cuando queremos saber quien compuso una obra o canción)
You're kidding! – ¿estás bromeando? *(usamos esta expresión cuando estamos asombrados y no creemos lo que nos están diciendo o cuando es algo difícil de creer)*

Grammar – Gramática
Pronouns and adverbs – Pronombres y adverbios
Whatever – lo que sea / cualquier cosa
Whatever you say, it is fine with me – lo que sea que digas, está bien por mí.
Whoever – quien sea – cualquier persona
Whoever comes first will get the prize – cualquiera que llegue primero recibirá el premio.
Whenever – cuando sea / en cualquier momento
Whenever you come, I'll be here waiting for you – cuando sea que vengas, estará aquí esperando por ti.
Wherever – donde sea / en cualquier lugar
Wherever you are, I hope you are happy – en donde quiera que estés, espero que estés feliz.
También puedes usarlos al dar órdenes; cuando esto sucede, la orden o el mandato es más fuerte de lo normal.
Whatever you do, don't mess it up – no importa lo que hagas, pero no metas la pata.
Whoever you marry, marry her for love – con quien sea que te cases, hazlo por amor.

Nivel Tres

Reflexive – Emphatic pronouns – Pronombres reflexivos y enfáticos.

Myself – yo mismo
Yourself – tú mismo
Himself – él mismo
Herself – ella mismo
Itself – él o ella mismo
Ourselves – nosotros mismos
Yourselves – ustedes mismos
Themselves – ellos / ellas mismas

Como pueden ver, la palabra "*self* – *mismo*" convierte a los pronombres personales en pronombres reflexivos; y como aprendimos en la primera lección, el plural de "*self*" es "*selves*". No lo olviden.

Usamos estos pronombres para enfatizar e indicar que el sujeto efectuó la acción o que ha sido efectuada por uno mismo.

I learned English myself – aprendí inglés yo mismo *(nadie me ayudó)*.

The secretary herself finished the project – la secretaria misma terminó el proyecto *(ella misma, nadie más)*

He considered himself handsome – Él se considere hermoso.

When he was discovered, he shot himself – cuando lo descubrieron, se dio un tiro.

They gave themselves a raise – ellos se aumentaron el sueldo.

A veces usamos "by" o "all by" para enfatizar que nadie más ayudó o tomó parte en la acción.

I fixed the computer by myself – arreglé la computadora yo mismo.

I fixed the computer all by myself – arreglé la computadora yo solito *(nadie me ayudó)*.

Pronoun + of – Pronombre más of

Sabemos por lecciones anteriores el significado y uso de "of", solo vamos a agregar algunos pronombres con el patrón para que continuemos incrementando nuestro conocimiento.

One of them is crying – una de ellas está llorando. *(Cuando hay más de dos personas en el grupo)*

Neither of us is crying – ninguno de nosotros está llorando. *(Cuando solo hablamos de dos personas)*

Both of them are crying – ambas están llorando. *(Cuando hay dos personas nada más)*

All of you are crying – todos ustedes están llorando. *(Cuando hay tres o más personas en el grupo)*.

Some of them are crying – algunos de ellos están llorando. *(Cuando hay un grupo de más de three personas)*.

None of them are crying – ninguno de ellos está llorando. *(Cuando hablamos de un grupo de tres o más personas)*.

Adjectives – Adjetivos
Old - viejo
Own – propio (esta palabra siempre se usa después de un adjetivo posesivo my own money – mi propio dinero)

Nivel Tres

Poor - pobre
Excellent - excelente
Loose – flojo (lo contrario de apretado)
Sharp – filoso
Sore – adolorido (cuando se tiene dolor)
Tight - apretado
Crowded – lleno de gente (lleno de personas o cosas).

Regular verbs – Verbos regulares
To marry - married - married - casarse
To solve - solved – solved - resolver
To cure – cured – cured - curar
To drop – dropped- dropped – caer / dejar caer
To laugh – laughed – laughed - reír
To serve – served – served - servir
To stop – stopped – stopped - detener
To try on – tried on – tried on – probarse *(ropa)*
To arrange – arranged – arranged – organizar / arreglar
To camp – camped – camped - acampar
To drown – drowned – drowned - ahogarse
To hire – hired – hired – contratar / emplear
To sail – sailed – sailed - navegar
To smile – smiled – smiled - sonreír
To surf – surfed – surfed – surfear
To trouble – troubled – troubled – molestar / preocupar
To welcome – welcomed – welcomed – dar la bienvenida

Irregular verbs – Verbos irregulares

To mean – meant – meant – significar / querer decir

To spend – spent – spent - gastar

To cut – cut – cut - cortar

To fall down – fell down – fallen down – caerse

To grow – grew – grown – crecer

Get out of the way

There was no stopping Zack. Traffic lights didn't intimidate him. Potholes just made the road more interesting. He needed to feel the wind blowing his hair. Whoever got in his way was sorry. If the other lane was empty, he'd just pull over into the other lane and fly by. Honk, honk, he'd honk his horn. "Come on, move!" Then he'd follow closely behind the car until the driver pulled over and allowed Derek to get around him.

Zack's last glorious ride was on Memorial Day. From the on-ramp, he saw a couple cars in the right lane. He laughed and laid his foot on the accelerator. Vroom! The car shot ahead, and he merged into the right lane, just ahead of the other cars. The drivers had to brake to avoid an accident and neither of them was happy about it. They held their hands on the horn for a long time. "Whatever," Zack said and ignored them.

He went faster and faster. The trees were a blur. Suddenly, he saw another blur, a spot of color on the road. He switched lanes just in time to miss the hitchhiker. "I almost gave him a ride to remember,"

Zack thought. He came up to the horse farm. He slowed down a little to look at the white-fenced fields. He wasn't looking at the road when he saw someone run off the road. Another near miss. "Wow, I've got to slow down," he thought. He went a little slower until he passed the commercial district. As he passed the mall, he started to accelerate again when he saw a boy in the road. "What on earth?" he said and swerved to miss him. After all of these mishaps, he asked himself if he should slow down. But he soon forgot and got back into his normal mode of driving. That's when he heard the siren. He looked in the rearview mirror and saw the flashing lights. "Darn," he said. He slowed down and pulled over onto the shoulder.

"In a hurry?" the policeman asked him. He tried to laugh, but he realized this was going to be a very expensive ticket. "Let's see, going 90 in a 60-mile zone. That's over $300." Zack said nothing, hoping the policeman would consider him respectful and lower the fine. No luck. The policeman handed him a citation and returned his papers.

Back home, Zack called his friend Martin, a lawyer. "What should I do?"

"Go to court. Say you were just going with the flow of traffic. Maybe he'll reduce your fine. And no jokes!"

Exercises – Ejercicios

Exercise 1.1: Add a reflexive/emphatic pronoun to each of the following sentences.

Example: My brother painted the portrait _himself_.

I _____ don't eat much fruit.

They had to build the house _____.

We're going to write the manual _____.

The dog _____ showed rescue workers where to find its owner.

You should talk to her _____ and explain the misunderstanding.

Exercise 1.2: Write *whatever, whoever, whenever,* or *wherever.*

Example: _Whenever_ she comes, I'll heat her food.

You can come _____ you want.

_____ you are, you can get in touch with our customer service.

_____ money she makes, she spends.

You can marry _____ you want.

I'll eat _____ you give me.

Exercise 1.3: Write the letter of the answer.

_____ Do you want chicken or beef?

_____ Did you like your teachers in college?

_____ Did the students pass the class?

Nivel Tres

_____ Will you take your books with you?

_____ Which of your boys plays soccer?

a. Yes, some of them did.
b. I want both of them.
c. Neither of them is involved in sports.
d. Well, one of them was really amazing. The rest were okay.
e. Yes, I'm going to need all of them.

Exercise 1.4: Complete the texts. Write the appropriate phrase from below.

by the way   come on   help yourself   take
care   you're kidding

Of course, I'll remind you. Ah, _____,
don't forget to call Dad.
Oh, there's plenty of food in the fridge.

_____!
Do you have to leave? We'll miss you. Oh, all right.

_____.

He left your sister? _____.
He seemed so in love.

Oh, _____. Please! I really need your help!

25

Lesson 2
To run out of gas – Quedarse sin combustible

Conversation

"I'll be right back, Honey. I'm going to go get the rental car for our trip," John called to his wife.

"Okay," Trisha replied. "Don't forget anything. What did they say you need?"

"Let's see, my driver's license, insurance policy, credit card, of course, and, well, any cash in case I don't want them to charge the deposit to the card."

"You don't need any other ID?" she asked.

"They didn't mention any."

"Okay, I'll have the suitcases ready when you get back."

When John came back with the car, he checked it over to make sure it was ready for the trip. Then, he packed up the car, and they started their trip from Tennessee to Texas. The first day was uneventful. They stayed overnight at a hotel and drove for another ten hours when the car stopped in the middle of the road. John pushed it to the side of the road and checked everything—the oil and water, of course, the carburetor, the radiator. Everything seemed okay. He called his insurance company for roadside assistance. When the man checked the car over, he laughed and said, "I could tow you to the gas station over there by the off-ramp."

"Seriously?" John asked. "Sorry about that. I could've just walked there, I guess. I didn't realize it was just the gas! Can you just give me a ride there and back?"

"Sure," the driver replied. "Now that I'm here, I might as well be of some use to you." The tow truck driver made sure John had an approved gas can and gave him the promised ride.

New words – Nuevas palabras
Ambulance - ambulancia
Battery - batería
Carburetor - carburador
Deposit - deposito
Dirt - sucio
Engine – motor (de vehículo)
Gas - gas
Including – incluyendo
Insurance - seguro
Kilometer - kilómetro
Noise - ruido
Oil – aceite / petróleo
Plus - más
Radiator - radiador
Service station – estación de servicio
Spare – llanta de repuesto, neumático
Tank - tanque
Tire – llanta / neumático
Trunk – cajuela / baúl
Warranty - garantía

Nivel Tres

Wheel – volante / rueda / timón
Chance - oportunidad
Contract – contrato
Desk - escritorio
Drawer – gaveta / cajón
Experience - experiencia
Fair – feria / justo
Marketing – mercadotecnia
Matter - asunto
Message - mensaje
Order – orden
Until - hasta
Report - reporte
Bomb - bomba
Cameraman - camarógrafo
Explosion - explosión
Floor – piso / suelo
Guy – tipo (hombre)
Helicopter - helicóptero
Hijacker - secuestrador
Hijacking - secuestro
Passenger - pasajero
String – cuerda / hilo

Words Definitions
All over: when you have finished something, we say "it is all over." "It is over" is the same as saying "it is finished." It also means "everywhere."
Fair: An event or place where companies gather to show their products to public view.
Insurance: when you buy a vehicle, you go the

insurance company to buy the insurance, so if you have an accident, they will pay for the damages over/beyond the deductible.

Matter: *when there is something important to discuss. However, in conversation you say, "What's the matter?" which is the same as "What's the problem?"*

Pleased: *when you are happy about something. You are satisfied.*

To keep warm: *when you help something or someone to keep warm or the same temperature; you can use "to keep" with many adjectives.* to keep cold, to keep happy, etc.

Warranty: *when you buy something, you might get a warranty, meaning that the manufacturer will fix certain types of problem you might have with the appliance in the next few months or years.*

Phrases and Expressions - Frases y expresiones
Do as I say – haz como yo digo *(haz como te digo)*
To get hurt – lastimarse / salir lastimado
Listen – escucha *(cuando queremos que alguien nos mire o preste atención)*
Look here – mira aquí / Oye tú / usted *(cuando queremos que nos miren y presten atención)*
Or else – si no *(es una expresión de advertencia, hace lo que digo o si no, ya veras, te atienes a las consecuencias)*
To pay attention – prestar o poner atención
Shut up – cállate / no hables *(no es cortés)*
Smart aleck – sabelotodo – sabiendo *(cuando*

alguien no está haciendo lo que le dijimos que haga.
No es una buena palabra, y frecuentemente indica
que la persona has sido irrespetuosa con alguien de
autoridad, mayor o un experto en el area)

Thank goodness – gracias a Dios *(cuando estamos*
contentos de que algo haya pasado)

To be in – estar en *(cuando estamos en la casa, en*
la oficina, iglesia).

To be out – no estar en *(cuando no estamos en la*
casa, oficina, iglesia)

To give someone a chance – darle una oportunidad
a alguien.

To have a seat – tomar asiento

Let me see – déjame ver *(estamos diciéndole a la*
otra persona que nos espere mientras verificamos)

To let someone know – hacerle saber algo a
alguien *(decirle algo a alguien)*

Tell him I am here – dile que estoy aquí

On time – a tiempo

See you later – nos vemos después / más tarde

Damn – diablo / *coño (esta expresión no es buena,*
a muchas personas no les gusta decirla ni escucharla.
Solo cuando se está demasiado enfadado se podría
decir está frase)

Fill it up - llénalo

In 5 minutes – en 5 minutes

In fact – de hecho / en realidad

It depends – depende / eso depende

To run out of – quedarse sin / acabársele algo /
agotarse algo

Grammar – Gramática

Forms of "Can" and "To be able to" – Formas de "Can" y "To be able to".

Can: solo tiene dos formas "*can / can't*" y "*could / couldn't*". Como ya habíamos explicado, "*can*" es para el presente simple y "*could*"es para el pasado simple y el condicional. Siempre lo usamos con otro verbo.

I can work hard now – puedo trabajar duro ahora.

I could work hard when I was young – pude trabajar duro cuando era joven.

También usamos "can" para referirnos al futuro.

I can come tomorrow – puedo venir mañana.

I cannot go to church on Sunday – no puedo ir a la iglesia el domingo.

Usamos "could" también como ya hemos aprendido en la forma cortés de "can" para pedir permiso. En este caso significa lo mismo que "may".

Can I talk to you? - ¿puedo hablar contigo?

Yes, you can. – Sí, puedes.

No, you can't. – No, no puedes.

Could I talk to you? – ¿podría hablar contigo?

Yes, you could. – Sí, podrías.

No, you couldn't – No, no podrías.

May I talk to you? - ¿puedo hablar contigo?

Yes, you may. – Sí, puedes.

No, you may not – No, no puedes.

Usamos *"To be able to – ser capaz de / poder hacer algo / tener la capacidad de"* con otro verbo in infinitive (esto es con "to"). Podemos usarlo en cualquier tiempo o forma.

I am able to travel – puedo viajar / tengo la capacidad para viajar.

I wasn't able to travel – no podía viajar / no tenía la capacidad para viajar.

I didn't use to be able to travel – no solía poder viajar.

I've been able to travel – he sido capaz de viajar / he podido viajar.

I'll be able to travel – podre viajar

I am not going to be able to travel – no poder viajar / no tendrá la capacidad de viajar.

I wouldn't be able to travel – no sería capaz de viajar.

When to use "can / could / to be able to" – Cuando usar "can / could / to be able to".

Usamos "can / could / to be able to" para decir que tenemos la habilidad o posibilidad.

She can sing – ella puede cantar *(habilidad)*.

She is able to sing – ella puede cantar / ella tiene la capacidad para cantar *(habilidad)*

She couldn't sing – elle no pudo cantar *(habilidad)*

She wasn't able to sing – ella no pudo cantar *(habilidad)*

She can probably sing – probablemente ella puede cantar *(posibilidad)*

She will probably be able to sing – ella probablemente podrá cantar *(posibilidad)*.

She probably couldn't sing – probablemente ella no pudo cantar *(posibilidad)*.

She probably wasn't able to sing – probablemente ella no pudo cantar *(probabilidad)*.

Recuerden que podemos o no usar la palabra "probably" en la oración y el significado vendría siendo el mismo; sin embargo, tiene mejor sentido cuando la usamos.

Para pedir permiso usamos "Can" o la forma cortés "could / may". Nunca usamos "to be able to" para permiso.

Forms of "must" and "have to" – Formas de "must" y "have to".

La palabra "must" solo tiene una forma y la usamos solo para referirnos al presente o futuro.

I must fix the car now – debo arreglar el carro ahora.

I must fix the car tomorrow – debo arreglar el carro mañana.

Podemos usar "to have to" en todos los tiempos y formas.

I have to fix the car now – tengo que arreglar el carro ahora.

I am going to have to fix the car tomorrow – tendré que arreglar el carro mañana.

I didn't have to fix the car – no tuve que arreglar el carro.

Recuerden,

En la forma negative "*mustn't*" y "*don't have to*" tienen diferente significados.

You mustn't fix the car now – no debes arreglar el carro ahora *(you may not fix the car now)*

You don't have to fix the car now – no tienes que arreglar el carro *ahora (you don't need to fix the car now – no necesitas arreglar el carro ahora)*.

No olviden que el "*must*" es un fuerte mandato, que hay que hacer la cosa si o si, mientras que "*have to*" tienes que hacerlo, pero también puede que no lo hagas.

The Adverb "Back" – El adverbio "back".

Podemos usar el adverbio "back – atrás, detrás" con muchos verbos. Veamos algunos.

To give back – devolver / dar de vuelta.

Give me my watch back – devuélveme mi reloj.

To want back – querer de vuelta.

I want my money back – quiero mi dinero de vuelta.

To need back – necesitar de vuelta.

I need you back – te necesito de vuelta – necesito que regreses.

To go back – retornar.

Go back the same way you came – retorna o regresa por el mismo camino que viniste. *(Cuando quien habla no está en el lugar de destino)*

To come back – regresar / retornar.

Come back, please. I cannot live without you – por favor, regresa. No puedo vivir sin ti. *(Cuando la persona que habla está en el lugar de destino).*

To take back – retornar / devolver.
Take the money back – regresa el dinero / devuelve el dinero.

To bring back – traer de vuelta – retornar.
Bring me my dog back, please – regrésame mi perro, por favor /tráeme mi perro de vuelta, por favor.

To walk back – regresar caminando.
I cannot walk back, it is too far – no puedo regresar caminando; es demasiado lejos.

To run back – regresar corriendo.
I ran back to the house when I heard the news – regrese corriendo a la casa cuando escuche la noticia.

To drive back – regresar conduciendo.
I must drive back to the service station for gas – debo regresar conduciendo a la estación de servicio por gas.

Indirect Commands – Órdenes indirectos.
"Don't use my perfume!" Tiffany's father said – Tiffany's father *told her not to use* his perfume. – "No uses mi perfume," dijo el padre de Tiffany. – El padre de Tiffany le dijo que no usara su perfume.

"Brush your hair, Yeiris!" her mother said – Yeiris mother *asked her to* brush her hair. – "Cepillate el cabello, Yeiris," dijo su madre – La madre de Yeiris le dijo que se cepillara el cabello.

"Please do it as quickly as possible," he said to me – He *asked me to do* it as quickly as possible. – "Por favor, hazlo lo más pronto posible," me dijo él – Él me pidió que lo hiciera lo más pronto posible.

Como pueden ver, estamos usando *"told- dijo"* y *"asked – pidió"* para expresar una mandato de una tercera persona. Es lo mismo que en español. Recuerden, cuando el mandato es negativo, el *"not"* vienes antes del *"to"*.
"Don't worry," Hector's father said. Hector's father told him not to worry – No te preocupes, dijo le dijo el padre de Héctor. El papá de Héctor le dijo que no se preocupara.

Reported Speech – Discurso indirecto

Cuando queremos decir lo que otra persona dijo sin usar sus palabras exactas, usamos el "reported speech".

Doctor Peter *says* you'll be fine – el doctor Peter dice que estarás bien.

He *says* he doesn't want it – él dice que no lo quiere.

Algunas veces usamos "that" para unir la oración, más parecido al español. Veamos los mismos ejemplos.

Doctor Peter *says that* you'll be fine – el doctor Peter dice que estarás bien.

He *says that* he doesn't want it – él dice que no lo quiere.

Es muy sencillo y fácil usarlo. Solo tenemos que recordar "says – dice" y a opción nuestra agregamos el "that – que" o no. Como prefiramos.

The president *says that* he'll solve the electricity

problem – el presidente dice que el resolverá el problema de la luz.

The girl *says* you are mean to her – la niña dice que eres malo con ella.

Conditional (type 1) – Condicional (tipo 1).

En inglés encontraremos diferentes tipos de condicionales con "if – si condicional", vamos a ver el primer tipo.

If – when – si condicional – cuando

Si o cuando algo pasa, algo más pasará.

You will be very happy *if* you come with me – serás muy feliz si vienes conmigo.

You will be very happy *when* you come with me – serás muy feliz cuando vengas conmigo.

She will be very sad *if* she goes with him – elle estará muy triste si ella se va con él.

She will be very sad *when* she goes with him – ella estará muy triste cuando se vaya con él.

Usamos el presente simple (no el futuro) después de "if" y "when".

If not - unless / either

Si algo no sucede o a menos que suceda, algo más sucederá. Recuerden que esta estructura es con el negativo. Son usadas para un condicional.

If you don't come, I won't talk to you – si no vienes, no hablaré contigo.

Unless you come, I won't talk to you – a menos que vengas, no hablaré contigo.

If she doesn't come, I won't give her the money – si ella no viene, no le daré el dinero.

Unless she comes, I won't give her the money – a menos que ella venga, no le daré el dinero.

También podemos usar "either... or" para describir la misma idea.

Either you come, *or* I won't talk to you – o vienes o no hablaré contigo.

Either she comes, *or* I won't give her the money – o ella viene o no le daré el dinero.

Either you come *or else*... - o vienes o te atienes a las consecuencias / o vienes o verás.

Conjunctions – Conjunciones.

Vamos a ver "*either... or*" y "*neither... nor*".

I'll finish the project. If I don't, John will – terminaré el proyecto. Si no lo hago, John lo hará.

Either Peter *or* I will finish the project. Lo termina Peter o lo termino yo.

En el negativo tenemos en español "*ni...ni*". Veamos.

You are not smoking. My father isn't either – No estás fumando. Mi padre tampoco.

Neither my father *nor* you are smoking – ni mi padre ni tú están fumando.

You not learning Spanish. My sister isn't either – No estás aprendiendo español. Mi hermana tampoco.

Neither my sister *nor* you are learning Spanish – ni mi hermana ni tú están aprendiendo español.

Normalmente usamos un verbo en plural después

de "*either... or / neither... nor*". Pero recuerden, cuando son usados como pronombres, entonces el verbo siempre estará en singular. *Either of them is* able to swim – cualquiera de ellos es capaz de nadar.

Neither of us wants to start – ninguno de nosotros quiere iniciar.

Recuerden, al igual que en español, cuando eres parte de la conversación y eres el hablante, siempre deberás contarte de ultimo; no es correcto decir "yo y María"... ¿verdad? Lo correcto es decir "María y yo". Lo mismo acontece en inglés.

Either he or *I* – o él o yo.

They saw him and *me* – lo vieron a él y a mí.

Adjectives – Adjetivos
Available – disponible
Flat – desinflado / rueda pinchada
Medium sized – talla mediana
Plenty of – suficiente de
Spare – repuesta / extra
Convenient - conveniente
Pleased - satisfecho
Urgent - urgente
Deaf - sordo
Frightened – aterrado

Regular verbs – Verbos regulares
To check – checked – checked – chequear / verificar
To fill – filled – filled - llenar
To return – returned – returned - regresar

Nivel Tres

To suggest – suggested – suggested - sugerir
To discuss – discussed – discussed - discutir
To arrest – arrested – arrested - arrestar
To belong – belonged – belonged - pertenecer
To hijack – hijacked – hijacked - secuestrar
To pray – prayed – prayed - orar
To pull – pulled – pulled - halar
To push – pushed – pushed - empujar
To reduce – reduced – reduced - reducir

Irregular verbs – Verbos irregulares
To be able / was (were) able / been able – ser capaz
To break down / broke down / broken down - dañarse
To blow up – blew up – blown up – explotar
To hold – held – held – mantener / sostener
To run away – ran away – run away - huir

The hijacking

Randy knew he couldn't turn back. If he changed his mind now, he would go to jail for sure. He tied up his prisoner as tight as he could and threw him into the truck. The prisoner yelled and yelled, making ridiculous threats: "If you don't let me go, I'm going to call the police! You are definitely fired. Either you let me go, or you're going to lose your insurance. You're not going to see another pay check, you hear me? And I won't recommend you for other jobs either."

Randy just laughed. He'd wanted to kidnap his

boss for a very long time. He enjoyed hearing the desperate pleas from the back of the truck. He took him out to a deserted cabin and locked him inside. The next day, he went to work as usual. He took his time on the **overdue** project. Around noon, he called his boss's home to ask about him. Then he reported the disappearance to the police: "I don't know what happened to my boss today. He didn't come in to work today. His wife said he didn't go home last night either. I'm a little worried about him."

After work, he wrote a ransom note and mailed it from the next town over. Then he waited. No money came. He had to go out and feed his boss the next day or he would be sick. While he was there, he heard a helicopter. "Great!" he thought. "They've seen my truck and will know it's me." But he had something else up his sleeve. He worked feverishly for a few minutes, and when the police arrived outside and demanded that he come out, he yelled, "I've got a bomb!" He set the timer and sneaked out the back window. As he ran, the trees and brush scratched his face and tore his clothes, but he was nearly a mile away when the bomb went off. He felt a little worried for his boss and his wife, but he comforted himself saying, "At least I won't have to finish my project today." Then he heard another explosion. He had only set one bomb. What was that noise? Again and again, he heard the explosions. He opened his eyes and saw the alarm clock. "No," he yelled as he jumped out of bed to get ready for work.

✎ **Exercises – Ejercicios**

Exercise 2.1: Write the correct form of *can, could,* or *be able to.*

Cats _____ swim. (can)

Fish _____ fly. (can not)

The computer repairman _____ repair your computer. (be able to—past tense)

Your son _____ become a great singer. (could)

She has _____ finish the report. (not be able to)

Monkeys _____ climb. (can)

My mom _____ bake your wedding cake. (could)

I'm sorry, but I will _____ go to your wedding. (not be able to)

Exercise 2.2: Write "A" if the sentence shows ability, "P" for probability, and "A/P" for both ability and probability (if it's ambiguous).

_____ They couldn't help us escape.

_____ My boyfriend can lift an 85-pound bar 8 times!

_____ The company wasn't able to hide its criminal activity.

_____ She couldn't make soft chocolate chip cookies at high altitudes.

_____ They couldn't make it to the party.

_____ The girl wasn't able to give birth until she had a C-section.

_____ Can she type 70 words a minute?

_____ Nobody is able to live without sleep.

_____ Could this drink contain poison?

_____ I could never marry a pirate.

Exercise 2.3: Underline the correct verb.

I **need/run/come** my sewing machine **back**, please.

The boogieman **wanted/went/brought** the bad little boy **back** to his mother.

We had to **take back/give back/walk back** down the mountain.

She **needed/gave/went** the project **back** because she was too busy to do it.

They want you to **want/need/give** the car **back** since you didn't pay for it.

That terrible cat keeps **bringing back/coming back/giving back**.

Can you **take/go/want** the movie **back** to the store for me?

Some friends **went/drove/gave** us **back** to our house.

I **want/walk/come** the crib **back**, please.

She **gave back/wanted back/ran back** for the key.

Exercise 2.4: Make the direct speech indirect.

Policeman: "If you collect four of these tickets, you win a bicycle."

Teacher: "Bring pictures to class tomorrow."

Uncle Jerry: "You catch more flies with honey."

Veterinarian: "The best thing is to wash him."

Mechanic: "Your car will be as good as new."

Exercise 2.5: Write the verb in the correct form.

Do as I say, and nobody _____ hurt. (get)

If she arrives in time, we _____ her with us. (take)

When you fail a class, they _____ you come to summer school. (make)

Unless you stop him, Boris _____ the moose. (kill)

Either we save water, or we _____ enough for the summer. (not have)

Lesson 3
My coach – my star

Conversation

Max: Wow. I really don't feel like working tonight. I'm so tired.

Bobbie: But maybe we'll get to see Spark. Come on. I want to get his autograph.

Max: Oh, okay. But he might be too busy; you understand that, right?

Bobbie: Yes, of course, but I think this is our lucky night.

Max: Our lucky night?

Bobbie: No, not yours. Spark's and mine. He's going to score more goals than when he won the cup. And I'm going to get his autograph. It'll be worth a lot of money.

Max: Maybe. There have been lots of people who have gotten his autograph. He loves signing his name.

Bobbie: Yeah, I know, but not all tonight—his lucky night. He said he has the feeling he's going to play like never before. Now that he's back to work after his injury, he's going to really stomp on the other team.

Max: We'll see. I hope it's at least an interesting game so I have something to write about.

New words – Nuevas palabras
Autograph - autógrafo
Coach - entrenador
Condition – condición *(situación de salud)*
Crowd - multitud
Cup - taza
Field - campo
Goal – gol *(cuando se mete un gol al jugar)*
Interview - entrevista
Kiss - beso
Opportunity - oportunidad
Pay - paga
Pollution – contaminación
Position – posición *(puesto en una compañía)*
Sleeve – manga *(de la camisa)*
Sport - deporte
Team - equipo
Trash - basura

Words Definitions
Never mind: it is the same as saying "forget it," that's all right.

Condition: when something or someone is healthy or in good state of health.

True: when something is real. What really happened, is happening or will happen.

Deep down: in your heart. Expressing how you really feel about something. You can also say down deep.

Sweet: something that is not sour - the opposite of

sour. *Also when someone is kind.*

Phrases and Expressions - Frases y expresiones
A bit – un poco
Day after day – día tras día
Deep down – en el fondo / en lo profundo
Down here (there) – aquí (allá) abajo
For the best – es lo mejor
For the worst – es lo peor
Good luck – buena suerte
Hour after hour – hora tras hora
Look who's talking – mira quien habla
Never mind – olvídalo / ya no importa
On the road – viajando / en la carretera / de camino
To feel that – sentir que / creer que
I feel that she is right – siento que ella está en lo correcto / creo que ella está en lo correcto.
To find that – encontrar que / pensar que
I find that hard to believe – creo que eso es difícil de creer – para mí es difícil creerlo.
To fix up – hacer que algo o alguien luzca bien o lindo. Reparar una relación.
To go back to work – regresar al trabajo
To make friends – hacer amigos
To make up your mind – decidirte *(cuando no estás seguro y tienes que tomar una decisión)*
Up here (there) – aquí (allá) arriba
What do you say? - ¿Qué dices? / ¿Cómo ves? / ¿Está bien? *(cuando buscamos la aprobación de alguien)*

Grammar – Gramática
The auxiliary "May" and "Maybe" – El auxiliar
"May" y "Maybe".

En lecciones pasadas hemos aprendido como usar
"may"; veamos un poquito más de lo que ya hemos
aprendido y tomemos nota de este corto repaso.
Algunas veces cuando usamos "may", puede
significar "*maybe – tal vez*" o "*perhaps – tal vez*".
Recuerden, "*maybe*" y "*perhaps*" significan lo mismo.
Veamos.

Are you going to travel? - ¿vas a viajar o viajarás?
I may – puede que sí
I may not – puede que no.
I may travel – puede que viaje
I may not travel – puede que no viaje
Maybe I will – tal vez lo haré
Maybe I won't – tal vez no lo haré

Do you know if she's coming tonight? - ¿sabes si
ella vendrá esta noche?
She may – puede que sí
She may not – puede que no
Maybe she will – tal vez lo hará
Maybe she won't – tal vez no lo hará
O simplemente pueden contestar
Maybe – tal vez
Perhaps – a lo mejor, quien sabe
Recuerden, solo hacemos preguntas con "may"
cuando estamos pidiendo permiso. May I come in? -
¿puedo entrar?

"There is / are" with auxiliary verbs – "There is / are" con verbos auxiliares.

Usamos "there is" y "there are" en todos los tiempos y con verbos auxiliaries.

There may be a party tomorrow – puede que haya una fiesta mañana.

There used to be parties every week, but *there haven't been* any in a long time – solían haber fiestas todas las semanas, pero no ha habido ninguna en mucho tiempo.

There weren't any last month, and I don't believe *there'll be* any this month – no hubo ninguna el mes pasado y no creo que habrá ninguna este mes.

There can't be a party tomorrow, and *there aren't going to be* any this weekend – no puede haber una fiesta mañana y no habrá ninguna este fin de semana.

Fíjense bien en cada uno de los ejemplos resaltados. Es bastante sencillo, usen casi todos los tiempos para que tengan una mejor idea.

Verbs plus "ing" form – Verbos más la forma "ing".

Ya sabemos que la forma "ing" equivale al gerundio "ando – iendo". Algunos verbos y expresiones en inglés usan el "ing" después del verbo principal. En español sería como usar el infinito después del verbo principal. Veamos.

To enjoy - disfrutar

I *enjoy playing* cards – disfruto jugar cartas.

Fíjense bien: el primer verbo esta conjugado y el segundo verbo está con el "ing", mientras que en español usan el segundo verbo en infinito. Continuemos viendo más ejemplos.

To finish – terminar
We haven't *finished discussing* the situation yet – aún no hemos terminado de platicar la situación.
Tenemos "finished" en pasado y el próximo verbo con "ing".
I *finished talking* to you – terminé de hablar contigo.

To stop – detener / parar
Stop drinking, please – para de beber, por favor.
Please *stop running* away – por favor, deja de huir.

To be used to – estar acostumbrado
I *am used to waking up* early – estoy acostumbrado a levantarme temprano.

To get used to – acostumbrarse
I'll never *get used to getting* up so early – nunca me acostumbraré a levantarme tan temprano.

To feel like – sentir que
I *feel like eating* an apple – tengo ganas de o se me antoja comerme una manzana.
I *feel like taking* a shower – tengo ganas de tomar una ducha.

To have trouble – tener problemas
You'll always *have trouble trusting* people – siempre tendrás problemas para creer en las personas.

You'll never *have trouble finding* a job – nunca tendrás problemas para encontrar trabajo.

To think of – pensar en
I'm *thinking of opening* a new business – estoy pensando en abrir un nuevo negocio.
We're *thinking of traveling* to Italy – estamos pensando en viajar a Italia.
I'm *thinking of planning* a trip – pienso planear un viaje.

Algunos verbos especiales pueden llevar tanto el infinitivo como el "ing".
To begin – empezar
Suddenly she *began to cry* – de repente ella empezó a llorar.
Suddenly she *began crying* – de repente ella empezó a llorar.
They *began to play* cards – ellos empezaron a jugar cartas.
They *began playing* cards – ellos empezaron a jugar cartas.

To start – comenzar
When I told the story, they *started to laugh* – cuando les conté la historia comenzaron a reírse.
When I told the story, they *started laughing* – cuando les conté la historia comenzaron a reírse.

To like – gustar
I *like fishing* – me gusta pescar
I *like to fish* – me gusta pescar

She *likes cooking* – a ella le gusta cocinar
She *likes to cook* – a ella le gusta cocinar.

To prefer - preferir
I *prefer eating* fruit – prefiero comer frutas
I *prefer to eat* fruit – prefiero comer frutas
We *prefer running* – preferimos correr
We *prefer to run* – preferimos correr.

Como pueden ver, la estructura es fácil y sencilla; ustedes pueden usar cualquier de las dos formas.

Tenemos que prestar mucha atención al verbo "*to stop*", porque cuando le sigue un verbo en infinitivo significa una cosa y cuando es "*ing*" significo otra cosa. Veamos los ejemplos.

I stopped working – *paré de trabajar* (significa que estaba trabajando y me detuve)

I stopped to work – *me detuve para trabajar* (significa que estaba haciendo algo y lo dejé para trabajar).

She *stopped smoking* – ella dejó de fumar
She *stopped to smoke* – ella se detiene para fumar.

Reported Speech in Present and Past – Discurso indirecto en presente y pasado.

En la lección anterior, vimos el "reported speech"; vamos a ver un poco más sobre el tema.

Recuerden que algunas veces usamos "that" como ya aprendimos, pero es opcional; no es un deber.

My teacher says, "*You train* very hard" – Mi profesor dice, "Tú entrenas muy duro".

My teacher says that I train very hard – mi

profesor dice que yo entreno muy duro. Cuando el verbo principal "say / tell" está en pasado, el verbo del discurso indirecto a menudo está en pasado también.

She said, "*I want* a room" – ella dijo, "yo quiero una habitación".

She said (that) she wanted a room – ella dijo que quería una habitación.

Usamos el presente en el discurso directo, y el pasado en el discurso indirecto.

He used to say, "*You are* the best" – él solía decir, "Tú eres el mejor".

He used to say (that) I was the best – él solía decir que yo era el mejor.

Usamos el presente del verbo "to be" en el discurso directo, y el pasado del verbo "to be" en el discurso indirecto.

Peter said, "Mary has to study hard" – Peter dijo, "María tiene que estudiar duro".

Peter said that Mary had to study hard – Peter dijo que María tenía que estudiar duro.

Usamos "has" en el presente del discurso directo, y "had" en el pasado del discurso indirecto.

Hector said, "Tiffany is going to France" – Héctor dijo, "Tiffany va para Francia".

Hector said that Tiffany was going to France – Héctor dijo que Tiffany iba para Francia.

Usamos el gerundio en el discurso directo, y el pasado gerundio en el discurso indirecto.

They said, "We can sing" – ellos dijeron, "podemos cantar"

They said that they could sing – ellos dijeron que podían cantar.

Usamos "can" en el presente del discurso directo, y "could" en el pasado del discurso indirecto.

Ben said, "I'll go to Europe" – Ben dijo, "iré a Europa".

Ben said the he would go to Europe – Ben dijo que iría a Europa.

Usamos "will" en el presente del discurso directo y "would" en el pasado del discurso indirecto.

Recuerden que siempre que usen "tell" deberán usar un objeto indirecto.

Hector told me, "I used to train very hard" – Héctor me dijo, "Yo solía entrenar muy duro".

Hector told me that he used to train very hard – Héctor me dijo que él solía entrenar muy duro.

Reported questions "ask" – Preguntas discurso indirecto "ask".

Presten mucha atención en el órden de las palabras.

Hector always asks, "How many points did you get?" – Héctor siempre pregunta, "¿Cuántos puntos sacaste?"

Hector always **asks how many points I got** – Héctor siempre pregunta cuantos puntos saqué.

Tiffany **asked**, "Why **is** he happy?" – Tiffany preguntó, "¿Por qué está él feliz?"

Tiffany **asked** why he **was** happy – Tiffany preguntó por qué él estaba feliz.

Cuando no hay ningún pronombre interrogativo, entonces tenemos que usar "if- si condicional".

Tiffany asked, "Do you like apples?" – Tiffany preguntó, "Te gustan las manzanas"

Tiffany **asked me if I liked** apples – Tiffany me preguntó si me gustaban las manzanas.

Adverbs – Adverbios
At first – al principio /al inicio / al comienzo
Definitely - definitivamente
Nicely – agradablemente, con finura, bien
At least – al menos
Especially - especialmente
Together – juntos
Nearly – casi

Adjectives – Adjetivos
Deep - profundo
Sweet - dulce
True – verdadero / genuino
Embarrassed – avergonzado
I am embarrassed by her behavior – me siento avergonzado por su conducta
Embarrassing - vergonzoso
Nervous - nervioso
Shy - tímido
Messy – sucio / desastroso
Neat – limpio / pulcro / ordenado / puro

Regular verbos – Verbos regulares

To burn – burned – burned - quemar

To mess up – messed up – messed up – desordenar / estropear / arruinar / ensuciar

To paint – painted – painted - pintar

To roast – roasted – roasted - asar

To straighten up – straightened up – straightened up – enderezar / ordenar

To ask for – asked for – asked for – preguntar por / pedir

To cheer – cheered – cheered – animar / alentar

To interview – interviewed – interviewed - entrevistar

To save – saved – saved – salvar / guardar

To score – scored – scored - anotar

To train – trained – trained - entrenar

To believe – believed – believed - creer

To decide – decided – decided - decidir

To deserve – deserved – deserved - merecer

To manage – managed – managed – organizar / lograr / administrar

To move – moved – moved - mover

To settle down – settled down – settled down – establecerse / resolver / sentar cabeza

Irregular verbs – Verbos irregulares

To freeze – froze – frozen - congelar

To hide – hid – hidden - esconder

To put away – put away – put away – guardar / retirar

To tear – tore – torn - rasgar

To throw away – threw away – thrown away – botar / arrojar / desechar

To wear out – wore out – worn out – gastar / desgastar

To teach – taught – taught - enseñar

Pollution

News Anchor: We'll turn now to the local news. According to polls, Mr. Thompson is in the lead for the office of mayor. His campaign is based on cleaning up the city with the slogan "Cleaner politics, a cleaner city." In fliers and TV ads, you can see him at points all around town picking up trash—in a designer suit— and supervising cleanup efforts at rivers and along roadways. He's always criticizing current politicians and public works projects for corruption and lack of transparency. However, Thompson recently refused to release records of his campaign funding and expenses. Many people have begun to question the sincerity of Thompson's "clean" politics. But he doesn't have direct answers. Let's go now to this afternoon's interview:

Reporter 1: Mr. Thompson, many people are very excited about your campaign of cleaning up politics and cleaning up the city, but in spite of repeated requests for your funding records, nothing has been released. What explanation can you give us for this apparent contradiction in your message and practice?

Mr. Thompson: I'm glad to address this problem of cleaning up our city. Our society demands a general cleanup: a cleanup of politics and a cleanup of the parks, rivers, and streets. I am working to renew our city. You can depend on me.

Reporter 1: Mr. Thompson—

Mr. Thompson: Any other questions? I'm glad to answer your questions. Transparency is key for clean politics.

Reporter 2: Yes, Sir, some people have suggested that you may not really represent clean politics.

Mr. Thompson: There will always be people who criticize clean politics. They like talking about others so that no one will look at what they are doing. They arc afraid that their corruption will be exposed. You can count on me to expose dirty politics and clean up our dirty streets.

Reporter 3: Mr. Thompson, you have not been transparent. You have not released funding reports. You have not answered our questions. How can you call that clean politics?

Mr. Thompson: I have based my campaign on clean funding. You can always count on me to fight corruption. I will be accountable to taxpayers, unlike those who are in office now, who have not explained their use of taxpayer funds. I will publish spending budgets and expenses. We will bring transparency to our great city.

Exercises – Ejercicios
Exercise 3.1: Make the direct speech indirect.
"I love her," said Mark.
"This town is beautiful," they said.

"Where are you?" he asked.

"We're not going to throw away your toys," her parents promised.

"Go to sleep," he told his daughter.

"I score more points than any other player," the player said.

"There may be mice down here," John said.

"I find that hard to believe," said the policeman.

"Are you sure your husband will come?" the principal asked.

"Tom stopped to help the lady cross the street," Mac reported.

Exercise 3.2: Write the correct form of the verb. If two forms are possible, write both forms.

There used to _____ a park here (be).

We finished _____after closing time (eat).

I feel like _____ three coffees (drink).

The president may _____ over Christmas vacation (travel).

They're thinking of _____ a new cashier (hire).

Suddenly, it began _____ (rain).

A lot of people like _____ the sunset (watch).

I don't want to buy a membership. I prefer

_____ for one visit (pay).

My boss asked me _____ the project tonight (finish).

We stopped _____ the new museum on our way to our parents' house (visit).

Exercise 3.3: Write the correct form of the adjective or adverb.

She _____ asked me to wash my dishes (sweet).

She's a _____ girl (nice).

My brother is very _____ (neat).

Tim _____ stood outside the store (nervous).

They _____ lost their dog (definite).

Lesson 4

Spaceship travel – Viaje en la nave espacial

Conversation

Lizzie: What are you doing, Grandpa?

Grandpa: I'm working.

Lizzie: You're working? It looks to me like you're playing.

Grandpa: Playing? Playing with a rocket? With meticulous flight and landing plans? If that's what you call playing, I'm doing a good job of it.

Lizzie: You don't need to get angry, Grandpa. Have you planned how it will fly?

Grandpa: Have I planned—Lizzie, you are incredible. I have planned the flight time and return trip. I have planned how to avoid damage on reentry. I have even found a pilot.

Lizzie: A pilot?

Grandpa: Yes. Look!

Lizzie: It's my stuffed elephant.

Grandpa: Yes. They're supposed to be very intelligent. But that's just for aesthetics. I am finally going to realize my dream of breaking the sound barrier, of reaching other realms, of going beyond the ordinary limits imposed on frail humanity.

Lizzie: So where's the fuel kept?

Grandpa: Fuel?

Lizzie: Yeah, fuel. I mean, it has to have fuel to

fly, right?

Grandpa: Yes, of course. It's not quite—that is—I'm going to do that next.

New words – Nuevas palabras

Air conditioner – aire acondicionado (también se puede decir AC).

Amount – monto / cantidad

Astronaut - astronauta

Blood - sangre

Bone - hueso

Bowl – recipiente / taza / tazón

Brain - cerebro

Button - botón

Corn - maíz

Cotton - algodón

Cover – tapa / cobertura

Detail - detalle

Divorce - divorcio

Downhill – cuesta abajo *(en una colina)*

Dream - sueño

Earth – tierra

Energy - energía

Equipment – equipo

Except (that) – excepto (que)

Face - cara

Flour - harina

Frog - sapo

Fuel - combustible

Fur – piel *(tipo de ropa)*

Furniture - muebles

Nivel Tres

Glass – vaso / vidrio
Grape - uva
Hill – colina
History - historia
Invention – invento / invención
Journey - jornada
Leather – cuero / piel
Light – luz
Mess – lío / confusión / enredo
Metal - metal
Nylon - Nilo
Piece - pieza
Planet - planeta
Plastic - plástico
Rainstorm – tormenta de lluvia
Rat - rata
Reason - razón
Research – investigación
Scientist - científico
Ship - barco
Skin – piel
Sky - cielo
Snowstorm – tormenta de nieve
Space – espacio
Spaceship – nave espacial
Storm - tormenta
Strawberry - fresa
Tail – cola *(de un animal)*
Tractor - tractor
Vehicle – vehículo
Uphill – cuesta arriba *(en una colina)*

Way – forma / modo
Wheat - trigo
Witch - bruja
Wood - madera
Wool - lana
World - mundo

Word Definitions

Brain: what is inside our heads.

Can't stand: when you hate something or someone.

Fed up: when you are angry because something has happened more than once.

Good for nothing: when a person or thing never works.

History: events in the past.

Lazy: a person that doesn't like to work or do anything.

Stunning: when someone is very attractive.

Your honor: when we are speaking to a judge.

Way: how a person does something or goes somewhere.

Phrases and Expressions - Frases y expresiones

Can't stand – no soportar algo / odiar algo
Ever since – desde entonces
To fall asleep – caer dormido / dormirse
To get divorced (from) – divorciarse de alguien
To get to a point (where) – llegar a un punto en donde…
To get to the point (where) – llegar al punto donde…

Good for nothing – bueno para nada
I mean – quiero decir / esto es / es decir *(cuando queremos decir los mismo en diferente forma para explicar lo dicho o para justificar lo dicho)*
To lose a job – perder un trabajo
Off and on – de vez en cuando *(no muy a menudo)*
On purpose – a propósito / adrede
To put out a fire – apagar un fuego / detener el fuego
Your honor – su señoría
Good gracious – caramba / válgame Dios *(mostrando gran sorpresa por algo)*
For now – por ahora
Made from – hecho de *(refiriéndonos al lugar en donde se hizo)*
Made of – hecho de *(refiriéndonos al material de que está hecho)*
Means of transportation – medios de transporte
Off you go – listo para irte / ya puedes irte
Right here – aquí mismo
Right there – allá mismo
That's where you're wrong – ahí es donde te equivocas / ahí es donde estás equivocado.

Grammar – Gramática
Present perfect progressive – Presente perfecto continuo.

Este tiempo se usa más en inglés que en español. Usamos este tiempo cuando algo inició en el pasado, aún continúa pasando en el presente y puede que continúe en el futuro. Prestemos atención.

I've been waiting for you for five hours – he estado esperando por ti durante five horas *(comencé a esperar hacen five horas y aún sigo esperando)*

She *has been studying* since this morning – ella ha estado estudiando desde la mañana *(comenzó a estudiar en la mañana, aún está estudiando y puede que continúe estudiando).*

I've been studying for three hours, but *I've only studied* five pages – he estado estudiando por tres horas, pero solo he estudiado cinco páginas.

Normalmente no usamos el presente perfecto continuo con estos verbos: *to belong, to hate, to know, to like, to love, to remember, to understand.*

Using "can't be" and "must be" – Usando "can't be" y "must be".

Usamos "can't be" cuando pensamos que algo está incorrecto y "must be" para indicar que algo más es lo correcto.

You *can't be* only twenty. You *must be* at least thirty. No puede ser que solo tengas veinte. Tú debes tener por lo menos treinta.

She *can't be* working. She *must be* resting – no puede ser que ella este trabajando. Ella debe estar descansando.

Por supuesto, no siempre los usamos juntos.

I don't know who she is, but she *must be* the teacher. – No sé quién es ella, pero ella debe ser la profesora.

She was sleeping just a minute ago. She *can't be*

working. – Ella estaba durmiendo solo hace un minuto. No puede ser que esté trabajando.

The word "As" – La palabra "As"

Ustedes saben que usamos la palabra "as" para comparación (*I am as smart as you* – *soy tan inteligente como tú*). Ahora vamos a ver otros usos de "as".

Podemos usar "as" para significar *"while – mientras".*

I sing *as* I work – canto mientras trabajo.

I remembered the dog *as* I walked out the door – recordé el perro mientras salía de la casa.

Podemos usar "as" para significar *"because – porque".*

As we had no option, we had to break the door – porque no teníamos otra opción, tuvimos que romper la puerta.

As you left the keys in the car, we had to break the window – porque dejaste las llave dentro del auto, tuvimos que romper la ventana.

También podemos usar "as" como preposición delante de sustantivos y pronombres. En este caso "as" funciona como comparativo "like, similar to".

I used to work *as* a teacher, and all the students learned *like crazy* – solía trabajar como profesor y todos los estudiantes aprendían como locos.

She used to work *as a cook*, and anyone who tries her food, *eats like a horse* – ella solía trabajar como cocinera, y todos los clientes comían como animales (caballos).

Verbs of Sense and Perception – Verbos de sentidos y percepción.

Eyes – Ojos

To look at – mirar / observar

I was *looking at* you – te estaba mirando.

To look like – parecerse.

It *looks like* an apple – se parece a una manzana.

To watch – mirar / observar

I am *watching* TV – estoy mirando TV

To see - ver

I *saw* something strange – vi algo extraño.

Ears – Oidos

To listen to – escuchar

I was *listening to* the radio – estaba escuchando la radio.

To hear – oír

I *heard* people speaking – oí personas hablando.

To sound (like)

The music *sounded* very loud – la música sonaba muy alta.

It *sounded like* a disco – sonaba como una disco.

Nose – Nariz

To smell (like)

It *smells* good – huele rico.

She *smells like* flowers – ella huele como a flores.

Mouth – Boca

To taste – probar / saborear

It *tastes* delicious – sabe delicioso.

It *tasted like* an orange – sabía a naranja / tenía un sabor a naranja.

Fingers / Hands – Dedos / Manos
To touch – tocar o palpar
I *touched* your skin – toque tu piel.
To feel - sentir
It *felt like* heaven – se sintió como el cielo.
It *felt* warm – la sentí caliente.

También podemos usar "*to seem (like) – parecerse*" y "*to appear to be – aparentar ser o estar*" para describir cosas.
The sun *seems* hot today – el sol parece caliente hoy.
The sun *appears to be* hot today – el sol parece estar caliente hoy.
It *seems like* she's getting better – parece como que ella se está recuperando.
She *appears to be* getting better – ella aparenta como que se está mejorando.
También podemos usar "*to look like*" y "*to sound like*" para decir lo que pensamos sobre algo, como ya hemos visto anteriormente.
That *sounds like* a good idea – eso suena como una buena idea.
That *looks like* a good plan – eso parece un buen plan.

The passive voice – La voz pasiva
Usamos la voz pasiva cuando no sabemos quién hizo algo o cuando queremos enfatizar algo que fue hecho en vez de quién lo hizo. Recuerden, siempre habrá una forma en la voz pasiva para decir

exactamente lo mismo que lo que queremos expresar en la voz pasiva.

Active voice
Someone stole my dog – alguien se robó mi perro.

Passive voice
My dog *was stolen* – mi perro fue robado.
Si queremos indicar quien lo hizo en la voz pasiva, entonces usamos "by".
My dog *was stolen by someone* – mi perro fue robado por alguien.
The homework *was done by someone* – la tarea fue hecho por alguien.
Pueden usar la voz pasiva en todos los tiempos. Veamos algunos ejemplos.
My money *is kept* in the bank (present) – mi dinero está guardado en el banco.
My money *is being kept* in the bank (present progressive) – mi dinero está siendo guardado en el banco.
My money *was kept* in the bank (simple past) – mi dinero estaba guardado en el banco.
My money *will be kept* in the bank (future) – mi dinero será guardado en el banco.

The impersonal "you" – El "you" impersonal.
Cuando usamos "you" en una oración con sentido general, nos referimos a nadie en específico, más bien a todo el mundo.
You should speak English in class – se debe hablar

inglés en clase.
Everybody should speak English in class – todos deben hablar inglés en clase.
English should be spoken by everyone in class – el inglés debe ser hablado por todos en clase.
You can't smoke here – no se puede fumar aquí
Nobody can smoke here – nadie puede fumar aquí.
This place *can't be used for smoking* – este lugar no puede ser usado para fumar.
Como pueden ver, todas estas frases significan lo mismo; estamos usando el "you" en sentido general.

Adjectives – Adjetivos
Several - varios
Steady – estable / firme
Bright – brillante / claro
Close (to) – cerca de / junto a
I am close to the restaurant – *estoy cerca del restaurante.*
I am close to you – *estoy junto a ti.*
Dark - oscuro
Horrible - horrible
Incredible - increíble
Latest – lo más reciente / último
Ordinary – común / ordinario
Steep - empinado

Regular verbs – Verbos regulares
To design – designed – designed - diseñar
To equip (for / with) – equipped – equipped – equipar (para / con)

73

To export – exported – exported - exportar

To import – imported – imported - importar

To invent – invented – invented – inventar / crear

To manufacture – manufactured – manufactured – fabricar / manufacturar

To park – parked – parked - parquear

To pedal – pedaled – pedaled - pedalear

To produce – produced – produced - producir

To protect (from) – protected – protected – proteger (de)

To raise – raised - raised – criar / levantar

To appear – appeared – appeared – aparecer / parecer

To chuckle – chuckled – chuckled – reírse entre los dientes

To seem – seemed – seemed - parecer

To sound – sounded – sounded - sonar

To touch – touched – touched – tocar / palpar

To wonder – wondered – wondered – preguntarse / asombrarse / maravillarse

To develop – developed – developed - desarrollar

To divorce – divorced – divorced - divorciarse

To dream – dreamed – dreamed - soñar

To launch – launched – launched – lanzar / inaugurar

To snore – snored – snored - roncar

To test – tested – tested - probar / examinar

Irregular verbs – Verbos irregulares

To wind up – wound up – wound up – dar cuerda

To go on – went on – gone on – continuar /

avanzar / seguir
To light – lit – lit – encender / iluminar
To shake – shook – shaken – agitar / sacudir

The farm.

Farmer Joe has been trimming weeds in the grape vineyard for the past few days. He's hoping to finish today. He gulps down his breakfast and heads outside, his dog Lucky following behind him. An extension converts his tractor into a mechanical weed trimmer. But it's still really hard work. He throws some dry bread to his ducks and some of last year's hay to the goats. They gratefully reach out for a head scratch. Lucky growls, and Joe laughs.

This is Joe's favorite time to work. The sun over the horizon gives the grape leaves a yellowish hue. The cool, dewy air fills Joe's lungs, and the birds sound happy it's a new day. Lucky tries to shake the moisture off his feet, with no success. Joe checks the gas and scrapes dried weeds off the extension; then he powers up the tractor and heads out to the vineyards. Lucky runs before the tractor, avoiding the blades, then after the tractor, avoiding the wheels. As it draws near to lunchtime, Joe tries to get just a little bit more work done. There really isn't enough time in a farmer's schedule to pull the weeds, and even trimming them takes too long, but Joe hates using herbicides in his vineyards. And the freshly cut weeds smell heavenly.

When Joe goes inside, he finds his wife setting the

table. "Chicken salad today, with carrot sticks and chips," she tells him.

"Wonderful," he answers, washing his hands in the kitchen sink to avoid walking around the house and dropping weed clippings everywhere. He and his wife enjoy conversation over lunch, while Lucky looks through the screen door longingly. Then Joe goes back out to work some more. Working especially hard, he manages to finish weeding by six o'clock. He sets the timer on the irrigation system and heads inside for dinner. Lucky is hanging around on the deck, hoping for a bit of dinner. It's venison roast in mushroom gravy, and it smells good! The dog is finally in luck. Since there's banana cream pie for dessert, there will be a little extra meat for the dog.

Exercises – Ejercicios

Exercise 4.1: Write the correct form of the phrase: *can't be, must be,* or *seems like.*

Example: They _seemed like_ they were sincere. They were very generous.

The cake _____ gone! I just made it this morning.

You _____ tired. You haven't slept well all weekend.

It _____ I've seen her before. She looks vaguely familiar.

They _____ here already. It's supposed to take two hours to get here.

He _____ angry. He didn't say anything all evening.

You _____ so sad. He was a very sweet dog. I'm sorry he's gone!

It _____ made of plastic. It's too light to be metal.

She _____ my mother. I don't look anything like her.

It _____ they were impatient. Maybe they were planning to escape.

He _____ a nice guy. Invite him over so we can meet him.

Exercise 4.2: Complete the sentence. Write the verb in present perfect progressive.

My cousin _____ websites. He's very good at it! (design)

We_____ English teachers for ten years. (train)

That lime tree _____ much fruit lately. (not produce)

What's wrong with the dog? He_____
for thirty minutes. (shake)

My grandchildren _____ chickens!
(raise)

I_____ if you would tell him about
the burnt chicken. (wonder)

When will you take a break?

You_____ for six hours straight.
(paint)

Strange lights _____ above the house
at night. (appear)

You're still parking the car?

You_____ the car for ten minutes!
(park)

Please don't throw that out. I_____ it
for a project. (save)

**Exercise 4.3: Write the verb in the passive voice
and the tense given.**

Coffee _____ in more than fifty
countries. (grow-simple present)

Your purchase _____ on file for three
months. (keep-*will* future)

Apple tart _____ with apples, flour,
butter, and brown sugar. (make-simple present)

It looks like they're outside, but that movie

_____ in the studio. (film-simple past)

That brand _____ exclusively in the US, but not anymore. (produce—used to)

Yes, they _____ to the police. (report-present perfect)

🔒 Lesson 5
The state – El estado

💬 Conversation

Jim: Nothing ever changes.

Harry: Nope.

Jim: We've been cheated out of our hard-earned money for centuries.

Harry: Centuries.

Jim: And do we ever get anything for all that money?

Harry: Never.

Jim: No, we don't. And if we ask them what they did with it, they just make up a bunch of lies.

Harry: A bunch of lies.

Jim: They say things will change, but they're all the same.

Harry: All the same.

Jim: They say they'll save us money, but prices keep getting higher.

Harry: Higher and higher.

Jim: They say there will be more jobs, and instead unemployment increases.

Harry: Always increasing.

Jim: They say they'll improve health care, but they just keep taking away our benefits.

Harry: Yeah.

Jim: First, they take away our dental care and eyeglasses. And now we have to order our prescriptions through the mail or pay for them out of pocket. And if there is no generic, it takes forever to prove we absolutely need it.

Harry: Forever.

Jim: But what can we do?

Harry: There's nothing we can do.

Jim: If I were president, I'd—

Harry: What would you do?

Jim: Well, I'd—

Harry: Oh, come on.

Jim: Huh?

Harry: You'd be the same.

Jim: Yeah, I guess you can't do it all by yourself.

Harry: Can't do anything.

New words – Nuevas palabras

Advice - consejo

Chain - cadena

Government - gobierno

Health - salud

Inflation – inflación

Position – posición

Real estate – bienes raíces

Tax – impuesto / gravamen

Wealth – riqueza

Weekdays – días de la semana

Wish - deseo

Army – ejército

Nivel Tres

Chore – tarea – asignación
Couple - pareja
Event - evento
King - rey
Lawn – césped
Lawnmower – podadora / corta césped
Machine – máquina
Occasion – ocasión
Prince - príncipe
Princess - princesa
Queen - reina
Uniform - uniforme
Advantage - ventaja
Agriculture - agricultura
Candidate - candidato
Crop – cosecha / cultivo
Defense - defensa
Development - desarrollo
Education – educación
Election – elección
Information – información
Investment – inversión
Percent – porcentaje
Otherwise – de lo contrario / por lo demás / de otra
manera
Reward – premio
Strike - huelga
Unemployment – desempleo
Vote – voto
Voter – votante

Words Definitions

Advantage: a better chance or opportunity than someone else has.

Education: what you learn in school or at home. The teachings of your parents and teachers.

Election: a time when a country starts to select a new president. A time or process for selecting a candidate.

Inflation: when the cost of living goes higher.

Left: whatever still remains after everything or everybody is gone.

Occasion: a time for something or when something happens.

Strike: when people stop working because they want better conditions or are demanding something from the government or an institution.

Successful: when you have accomplished what you wanted to.

Tax: whatever money you have to pay to the government.

Uniform: special clothes people wear for school, work, or any institution.

Wish: something you want to happen.

Phrases and Expressions - Frases y expresiones

To break the news – dar las noticias de último minuto

In order to – para

*I went to your house **in order to** see you* – fui a tu casa para verte. *(Siempre le sigue un verbo)*

Worth it – lo vale / vale la pena

By hand – a mano *(hecho a mano)*
To leave someone alone – dejar a alguien solo *(no molestar a alguien)*
To make someone + adjective – hacer … a alguien. *(to make someone happy – hacer feliz a alguien). Siempre usaremos cualquier adjetivo para indicar lo que queremos decir.*
To stay after school – permanecer en la escuela castigado *(cuando ya todos se han ido y tú no puedes irte, porque estas castigado)*
To give away - regalar
To give trouble to – darle problemas a alguien
If I were you – si yo fuera tu
In a difficult position – en una difícil posición
What more…? - ¿Qué más?
Would rather – preferiría

Grammar – Gramática
Conditional type 2 – Condicional tipo 2.
Ya vimos y aprendimos el condicional tipo 1; ahora vamos a ver el tipo 2. Si algo pasó *(pero suponemos que no pasará)* o si algo fuera cierto *(pero suponemos que no es así)* entonces algo más pasaría.

If I had a lot of money, *I'd give* some of it away – si tuviera mucho dinero, regalaría parte de él.

I'd give some money away, *if I had* a lot of it – regalaría algo de dinero, si tuviera mucho.

En la forma condicional, usamos el pasado después de "if". Fíjense que la forma del verbo "to be" es "*were / weren't*".

If I were you, *I'd invest* in stock – si fuera tú, invertiría en la bolsa de valores. *(Aunque estamos hablando de "I", debemos usar "were" en este modo)*

She'd probably *hate* me *if she weren't* my wife – probablemente ella me odiaría si no fuera mi esposa. *(Aunque estamos hablando de "she", debemos usar "weren't" en este tiempo)*

También usamos "were / weren't" después del verbo "wish".

I wish she were here – desearía que ella estuviera aquí.

I wish he were in better condition – desearía que el estuviera en mejor condición.

El condicional de "can" es "could".

If I took the plane, *I could* get there on time – si tomaba el avión, podría llegar a tiempo.

Some uses of "would" – Algunos usos de "would".

Ya hemos visto cómo usar "*would*" en el condicional; veamos algunos otros usos. Algunas veces usamos "*would*" en lugar de "*used to*".

When I was young, I *would (used to)* walk to school every day – cuando era jóven, solía caminar hasta la escuela cada día.

I'd always *forget* my books when I was a kid – siempre olvidaba mis libros cuando era chico.

I always *used to* forget my books when I was a kid – siempre solía olvidar mis libros cuando era chico.

Algunas veces usamos "would" para indicar atención o prediccion en el pasado.

I knew she would tell you about it – sabia que ella

te lo diría.

Algunas veces hacemos énfasis en la palabra "would" para mostrar que esperamos que algo suceda y que no estamos contentos con eso o desaprobación por lo que consideramos una conducta típica.

You *would* do it, wouldn't you? – Lo harías, ¿o no?

The government *would* spend all our tax money on guns – el gobierno gastaría todo el dinero de nuestros impuestos en armas.

The verb "to wish" – El verbo "to wish".

Usamos "to wish" más el pasado para indicar como nos gustaría que sean las cosas.

We *wish (that) we were* pretty – desearíamos que fuéramos hermosas.

She *wishes she had* a car – ella desearía tener un carro.

Don't you wish that you didn't have to work? - ¿no desearías que no tuvieras que trabajar?

Usamos "to wish" más "would" para indicar como nos gustaría que las cosas cambien.

I wish he wouldn't smoke in the house – desearía que él no fume en la casa.

I wish it wouldn't rain so much – desearía que no lloviera tanto.

She wishes you would listen to her – ella desearía que tú la escucharas.

The passive voice – La voz pasiva

Ya aprendimos como usar la voz pasiva; vamos a ver la voz pasiva en pasado simple en contraste con el presente perfecto.

Recuerden que el pasado simple habla de un tiempo finito o de una acción terminada. El presente perfecto habla de un tiempo indefinido o de una acción que puede aún estar pasando. Ambos tiempos pueden ser usados en la voz pasiva.

The president *was elected* last month – el presidente fue elegido el mes pasado. *(Tiempo definido)*

The president *has been elected* – el presidente ha sido elegido *(tiempo indefinido)*

A lot of teenagers *were arrested* during the strike – muchos jóvenes fueron arrestados durante la huelga.

A lot of teenagers *have been arrested* – muchos jóvenes han sido arrestados.

Fijense bien en la estructura y la diferencia entre ambos tiempos.

Nouns formed from verbs – Nombres formados de verbos.

Veamos cómo se forman algunos nombres o sustantivos usando los verbos como base.

To develop – desarrollar
Develop*ment* - desarrollo
To equip – equipar
Equip*ment* – equipo
To invest – invertir
Invest*ment* – inversión
To apply – solicitar
Applic*ation* - solicitud
To inform – informar

Inform*ation* – información
To invite – *invitar*
Invit*ation* – invitación
To elect – *elegir*
Elec*tion* – elección
To invent – *inventor*
Inven*tion* - invento
To suggest – *sugerir*
Sugges*tion* - sugerencia
Como pueden ver, conociendo un verbo podemos formar palabras usando ese verbo como base. Presten mucha atención al concepto y practíquenlo muy bien. No hay una regla directa para aprender este concepto; deberán prestar atención y aprender en el proceso.

Adverbs – Adverbios
Ever before – nunca antes / más que antes
We are studying more than ever before – estamos estudiando más que antes (más que nunca. Deben entender que no significa nada negative solo)
Anyway – de todas formas / de cualquier modo
Backward – hacia atrás
Forward – hacia adelante
Rather (than) – preferir
I'd rather go home – preferiría irme a casa (usamos would con rather)
I'd rather go home than stay here – preferiría irme a casa que permanecer aqui. (Usualmente usamos than despues de rather)
Therefore – por tanto / por lo tanto

Adjectives – Adjetivos
Alive - vivo

Dead - muerto

Foreign – extranjero

Necessary - necesario

Successful - exitoso

Worth – digno / de valor

Left – remanente / resto (lo que queda de algo)

Mad – loco / demente / furioso

Willing – dispuesto / complaciente

Regular verbs – Verbos regulares
To encourage – encouraged – encouraged – animar / alentar / estimular

To explain – explained – explained - explicar

To fire – fired – fired – disparar

To invest – invested – invested - invertir

To suppose – supposed – supposed - suponer

To wish (for / that) – wished – wished – desear (por / que)

To allow – allowed – allowed – permitir / autorizar / dejar

To bake – baked – baked - hornear

To dress up – dressed up – dressed up – vestirse / disfrazarse

To milk – milked – milked - ordeñar

To mow – mowed – mowed - podar

To agree (with) – agreed – agreed - acordar

To elect – elected – elected - elegir

To inform – informed – informed - informar

To offer – offered – offered - ofrecer

To organize – organized – organized - organizar
To plant – planted – planted – plantar / sembrar
To reelect – reelected – reelected - reelegir
To vote – voted – voted - votar

Irregular verbs – Verbos irregulares
To freeze – froze – frozen - congelar
To feed – fed – fed - alimentar
To let – let – let – dejar / permitir
To shoot – shot – shot – disparar / tirar / arrojar

Ancient times and nowadays.
Cinthia wished she could go back to the days of chivalry. She could imagine herself as a beautiful damsel in distress, waiting for her prince in shining armor to come and rescue her, just at the last possible moment. She was most captivated by these dreams when it was time to do her chores. She was Cinderella sweeping and mopping, cooking and washing. Never mind the fact that she had disposable cloths so she could sweep and mop at the same time, she bought frozen meals to save time on cooking, and she had a washing machine and dryer so she could do all the wash in a few hours.

As a little girl, Cinthia used to ride her dog around and pretend he was a pony. She would braid her hair with ribbons and practice royal etiquette with her dolls and stuffed animals. When she entered the room, all the bears stood up. She was addressed as "Your Highness." She walked with perfect posture and was careful not to talk too much. At meals, she always ate small amounts of food, she kept her mouth wiped clean with a napkin, and she never put her elbows on the table

As a princess, she wouldn't waste her time on menial tasks. She wouldn't even have to do her hair. Her meals would be cooked for her. Her house would be cleaned by servants. She would supervise household meals and finances. She might do some needlework or dance a little. She would never be bothered with dusting.

It wouldn't be near as much fun to be a modern princess. She'd have to do photo shoots and worry about always looking perfect. How do you look like a princess in a day when so many girls use makeup and designer clothes! She'd have to go around doing good works and avoid any possibility of scandal. But there would always be journalists who would make up rumors. Imagine your face on those cheap newspapers in the grocery aisle—or on TV! No, it would just be too much work. She sighed as she settled down with a latte to watch her favorite history program on TV. Life in medieval times must have been so much simpler.

Exercises – Ejercicios
Exercise 5.1: Write the correct form of the verb in the passive voice.

I _____ always _____ to follow my dreams (encourage—simple past).

The president _____ in a time of unemployment and inflation (reelect—simple past).

Nobody would eat the tomatoes that _____ in the garbage pile (plant—simple past).

He can't stay home. A birthday party _____ for him (organize—present perfect).

Unfortunately, your money _____ in an unstable company (invest—simple past).

Exercise 5.2: What is the meaning of *would* in each sentence: past intention, result of a wish, typical "bad" behavior, or used to.

_____ They said they would hire her if she made a small investment in the company.

_____ I'm not surprised you got stuck doing everything; she would "forget" to do her chores.

_____ I wish he wouldn't always talk about his work.

_____ That man! He would dump his garbage in front of my house.

_____ He would whistle when he had to go home in the dark.

_____ I wish she would study more.

_____ We would visit my maternal grandparents on Christmas Eve.

_____ When I went home, I thought I would have time to relax.

_____ They would have a garage sale every summer to get rid of the toys they didn't play with anymore.

_____ I wish you wouldn't make fun of me.

Exercise 5.3: Second conditional: write the verbs in the correct form.

If I _____ (have) a million dollars, I

_____ (buy) you a car.

If she _____ (be) here, she _____ (tell) you the truth.

If Mom _____ (try) the cake, she _____ (recognize) her secret recipe.

If they _____ (wear) coats, they _____

(not be) cold.

If the Smiths _____ (agree) to sell the farm,

their children _____ (cry).

Lesson 6
The mystery – El misterio

Conversation

Chuck: That was a great meal.

Frank: Thanks! I'm pretty good at pork chops.

Chuck: They were perfect—tasty and tender! So, how have you been?

Frank: Okay. Well, . . .

Chuck: What's the matter?

Frank: You're not going to believe me, but I think there's a ghost in the house.

Chuck: Seriously?

Frank: I can hear a baby crying in the house.

Chuck: All the time?

Frank: No, just at night. I think the previous owners had a baby and maybe it got sick or—

Chuck: Do you hear it all over the house?

Frank: No. Just in the dining room and bathroom. And when I turn the lights out, I see little lights flickering around the house.

Chuck: Hmmm. Let's see. Both of these rooms have windows facing that house over there. Do they have a baby?

Frank: I don't know—well, now, I think they do.

Chuck: So don't you think you might hear their baby crying?

Frank: Well, I thought it was closer. You think I'm just a superstitious old man, don't you?

Chuck: Superstitious? No. You're just hard of hearing, old man!

New words – Nuevas palabras

Bargain - ganga
Block – cuadra / bloque
Bottom – fondo / trasero
Brick – ladrillo / block
Furnace - horno
Garbage – basura / desperdicio
Garbage can – zafacón / bote de basura
Ghost - fantasma
The inside – el interior
The outside – el exterior
Owner - dueño
Plumbing - plomería
Roof – techo / tejado
Shopping center – centro comercial
Store - tienda
Top – cima / tope
Wiring - cableado
Argument – argumento / alegato
Coincidence – coincidencia
Cousin -primo
Crystal ball – bola de cristal
Fortune – fortuna / suerte
Fortune teller – adivino
Nonsense – disparates / majaderías
Prediction – predicción

Relative – pariente
Carpet - alfombra
Copy - copia
Elevator - elevador
Feather - pluma
File - archivo
File cabinet – archivero
Jam – mermelada / atasco (cuando un papel se atasca)
Jar – taro / frasco
Lock - candado
Watchman - vigilante
Photocopier - fotocopiadora
Safe – caja fuerte
Wastebasket – zafacón
Wire - cable

Word Definitions

Ahead of: something that is about to happen, something coming, something in front of.

Argument: when you have a fight using words only.

Block: in a square area, a block represents the space surrounded by four streets.

Finally: after waiting a long time for something and it arrives, after everything else, last. Used to introduce the last of a group or series"

Previous: the one before.

Silly: someone or something that is full of nonsense.

Superstitious: a person that believes all kinds of

tales and stories with no reason at all and is afraid of things because they might bring bad luck.

Unlucky: *someone who brings bad luck or someone that does not have good luck.*

Phrases and Expressions - Frases y expresiones

To ask someone over – invitar a alguien a tu casa

To clean up – asear / limpiar / enderezar / reformar

For example – por ejemplo

To give someone a bath – darle un baño a alguien

To go right – salir bien *(cuando algo sale bien)*

To go wrong – salir mal *(cuando algo sale mal)*

To make matters worse – empeorar las cosas

To come true – hacer o volverse realidad

To leave home – dejar tranquilo o solo a alguien, no molestar a alguien

To leave something to someone – dejarle algo a alguien.

Sometime – algún día *(en el futuro, alguna vez)*

To tell someone's fortune – leer la suerte a alguien

That's nothing new – eso no es nada nuevo *(no es sorpresa, eso siempre sucede)*

Can afford *(can't afford)* – poder costear *(no poder costear) / poder permitir (no poder permitir)*

For sale – en venta

To move in – mudarse *(cuando ingresamos o mudamos en una casa, apartamento, etc.)*

To move out – mudarse *(cuando egresamos, salimos de una casa, apartamento, etc.)*

Now and then – algunas veces *(no muy a menudo)*

A number of – un numero de *(varios)*

Such – tan *(you are such a fool – tú eres tan tonto. It is such a lovely evening – es una velada tan hermosa)*

Grammar – Gramática

To have + noun + past participle – To have + sustantivo + pasado participio.

Cuando no podemos hacer algo nosotros mismos, o no queremos, hacemos que alguien lo haga por nosotros. Ahí es cuando usamos la combinación con el verbo "to have – haber o tener". Veamos.

I always *have my nails done* at Tiffany's – siempre me hacen las uñas en Tiffany.

I never *have my hair cut* at Thomson's – nunca me corto el cabello en Thomsons.

Are you having your house redecorated? – ¿vas a mandar a redecorar tu casa?

I am *having a tooth pulled* – me van a sacar una muela.

Fíjense que siempre usamos el verbo "to have" más el sustantivo y después siempre el verbo va en pasado participio.

To need + ing – To need + ing

Algunas veces usamos "to need" más el presente participio en vez de la voz pasiva.

My house is dirty. It *needs painting* (it needs to be cleaned) – mi casa está sucia. Necesita pintura (necesita ser pintada).

My car is broken. It *needs servicing* (it needs to be

serviced) – mi carro está dañado. Necesita mecánica (necesita ser reparado)

Agreeing and disagreeing – Acuerdos y desacuerdos.

Vamos a aprender las variaciones cuando estamos de acuerdo con alguien, cuando no estamos de acuerdo y cuando no estamos seguros.

I think Kennedy will be reelected – creo que Kennedy será reelegido.

When you agree – cuando estás de acuerdo.

So do I – yo también

I do too – yo también

I am sure he will – estoy seguro que sí

I am absolutely positive he will – estoy completamente positivo que lo será

Oh, definitely – o, definitivamente.

Of course (he will) – por supuesto (él lo será)

When you disagree – cuando no estás de acuerdo.

I don't – no.

No, he won't – no lo será.

I don't think so – no lo creo.

Of course he won't – por supuesto que no lo será.

When you aren't sure – cuando no estás seguro.

Maybe (he will) – tal vez (lo será)

Perhaps (he will) tal vez (lo será)

He may – puede que sí.

Possibly – posiblemente

Probably – probablemente
I am not sure – no estoy seguro
I guess – supongo
I suppose so – supongo

I don't think he'll be reelected – no creo que será reelecto.
When you agree – cuando estás de acuerdo.
Neither do I – yo tampoco
I don't either – yo tampoco
I am sure he won't – estoy seguro que no
I am absolutely positive he won't – estoy completamente positivo que no lo será.
Oh, definitely not – o definitivamente no.
Of course he won't – por supuesto que no lo será.
When you disagree – cuando no estás de acuerdo.
I do – yo sí
Yes, he will – sí, él lo será.
Sure he will – seguro él lo será.
Of course he will – por supuesto que lo será.
When you aren't sure – cuando no estás seguro.
Maybe (not) – tal vez (no).
Maybe he won't – tal vez no lo será
Perhaps (not) – tal vez (no)
Perhaps he won't – tal vez no lo será
Possibly not – posiblemente no.
Probably not – probablemente no.
I guess not – supongo que no.

Conjunction "so that" – Conjunción "so that"
Usamos "so that" para indicar el por qué de algo.

Podemos usar el "so" solo; el "that" es opcional. Veamos.

Speak loud *so (that)* they hear you – habla alto para que te escuchen.

Speak softly *so (that)* they don't hear you – habla bajo para que no te escuchen.

I am making dinner *so (that)* you can eat – estoy haciendo la cena para que puedas comer.

La idea es la misma y podemos usarlo en cualquier tiempo.

Adverbs – Adverbios
Away (from) – lejos (de) (lejos de algún lugar)
Quite – muy (this is quite good – esto es muy bueno "very")
Abroad – fuera del país – en el extranjero
Absolutely – absolutamente
Possibly – posiblemente
Finally – finalmente

Adjectives – Adjetivos
Away (from) – lejos (de) (lejos de algún lugar)
Quite – muy (this is quite good – esto es muy bueno "very")
Abroad – fuera del país – en el extranjero
Absolutely – absolutamente
Possibly – posiblemente
Finally – finalmente

Regular verbs – Verbos regulares
To collect – collected – collected – cobrar /

recolectar

To disappear – disappeared – disappeared - desaparecer

To knock on – knocked on – knocked on - tocar

To manage – managed – managed – dirigir / manejar

To notice – noticed – noticed – notar / percibir

To own – owned – owned - poseer

To realize – realized – realized – darse cuenta / entender

To redecorate – redecorated – redecorated - redecorar

To service – serviced – serviced – dar servicio o mantenimiento a un aparato

To shop – shopped – shopped – comprar (en tiendas)

To predict – predicted – predicted - predecir

To empty – emptied – emptied - vaciar

Irregular verbs – Verbos irregulares
To build – built – built - construir

Constructions tools

Building a house is a complicated process. Once the land is purchased, the placement of the house and driveway can be planned. You will want to have the architect design the house so that water flows away from the foundation; the structure must be made to survive typical weather conditions for the region (for example, tornadoes, snow storms, or flooding), and windows placed to take advantage of sunlight. Make sure you decide first where you will need any special plumbing and wiring before you have the plans made. When the design is complete, you will need to get a building permit. You can request it yourself, or you can hire someone to supervise the project and get all necessary permits (septic, electric, plumbing, etc.).

Before building, you need to get insurance to protect the construction workers and the building. Then, the process of building can begin. First, the foundation is laid, with special attention to the natural flow of water across the land. The frame will probably be made with cement block and filled in with cement. Make sure the placement of the walls is square and level, and install the floor after having plumbing lines installed. Next, the walls will be framed and built according to the blueprint. The studs must be made level and then nailed in place.

You can purchase prefab roof trusses or have your builders put them together. If you are in a region that receives a lot of snowfall, make sure the roof can handle the increased weight of snow during a snowstorm. Protect the roof from moisture damage; then install siding, doors and windows. Finally, finish off the roof.

On the inside, install water and sewage pipes, the central cooling and heating system, electrical wiring and fixtures, and insulation. Then, install the ceilings. You can now add plumbing fixtures—toilets, sinks, and bathtubs, finish off the walls, and add flooring. After the building passes inspection, you can bring in your appliances and have the utilities turned on. And you're ready to move in! Enjoy filling in the spaces you visualized with your furniture, window treatments, and decorations!

☑ **Exercises – Ejercicios**
Exercise 6.1: Match the actions to the cause.

_____ Jorie had a part-time job

_____ She left her dog with her sister

_____ She spent the afternoon at her sister's house

_____ She bought some peanuts

_____ She waited until her husband got out of work
A. so she could save money on a taxi.
B. so he wouldn't be too lonely.
C. so she could pay for her daughter's music lessons.
D. so she could get a ride home with him.
E. so she wouldn't be hungry.

Exercise 6.2: Write a sentence using the structure (a) *needs* + gerund and (b) *have* + past participle.
Example:
paint + nails   _My nails need painting._ I'm going to have my nails painted.
hem + pants   _Mark's pants need hemming._ He is going to have his pants hemmed._

trimming + hair _____;

she's going to _____

repair + shoes _____;

I want to _____replace + tires

we want to _____

harvest + corn_____;

they plan to _____
dry clean + shirts

_____;

George is going to

_____

Exercise 6.3: Functions: complete the sentence according to the function in parentheses.

My aunt would never lie to me. (agree)

Of course _____.
Your teacher didn't complain about you. (disagree)

I am absolutely positive _____.
Were you here on time? (agree)

Oh, yes. _____ definitely _____.
The fair won't affect my business. (not sure) Well, I

guess _____.
Cats can't swim. (disagree)

Really? I think _____.
Koalas are pretty stupid. (agree)

Yeah, _____ probably _____.

Lesson 7
Telling the truth – Diciendo la verdad

Conversation

Mom: Where did you get those chips?

Mark: I found them.

Mom: That's dangerous! You can't eat food that you find lying around. It could be poisoned.

Mark: Well, I mean, I found $1, and I used it to buy the chips.

Mom: Oh, where did you find the dollar?

Mark: In front of the apartment building.

Mom: Was anybody standing outside?

Mark: Yes.

Mom: Did you ask them if they had lost some money?

Mark: No. I mean, they didn't look like very nice people.

Mom: Why didn't you cross the street to avoid walking by them?

Mark: Well, I was with my friend who lives in that apartment building.

Mom: Ah, and he didn't see the dollar bill?

Mark: No, I saw it after he went inside.

Mom: So you were alone with the bad people?

Mark: Just for a second.

Mom: But they didn't see you picking up the money?

111

Mark: No, they were distracted.

Mom: What were they doing?

Mark: I think they were selling drugs or something.

Mom: And you didn't report it to the police?

Mark: No.

Mom: We need to tell them that people sell drugs outside that building.

Mark: No, Mom. . . . I mean, it was probably just this one time.

Mom: Mark, are you sure you found that money?

Mark: Um, maybe not.

Mom: Where did you get it?

Mark: I took it from your purse. I'm sorry, Mom.

Mom: You have to be careful, Mark. If you start stealing and lying, it will become a habit. You'll become a slave to your bad habits, and who knows where you might end up? Stealing and lying affect your relationships. You'll attract the worst type of friends, and you might even end up in jail!

Mark: I'm sorry, Mom.

Mom: Well, why don't you wash the dishes so you can earn that dollar?

New words – Nuevas palabras
Choice – elección / opción / alternativa
Liar - mentiroso
Lie - mentira
Truth - verdad

Nivel Tres

Cause - causa
Cement - cemento
Group - grupo
Hammer – martillo
Hardware – ferretería
Nail - clavo
Lumberyard – maderería / almacén de madera
Opinion – opinión
Orphanage – orfanato
Pliers - alicates
Responsibility - responsabilidad
Saw – sierra / serrucho
Screw – tornillo / tuerca
Screwdriver - destornillador
Tool - herramienta

Word Definitions
Lie: when you say something you know that isn't true.
Lumberyard: the place where you buy wood
Tool: the things you need or use to repair or do something.

Phrases and Expressions – Frases y expresiones
After all – después de todo
How did it go? - ¿Cómo estuvo? / ¿Cómo te fue?
To make someone do something – hacer que alguien haga algo. *(Cuando hacemos que alguien haga algo que no quiere, por fuerza o insinuación)*
To have someone do something – hacer que alguien haga algo *(cuando hacemos que alguien*

haga algo voluntariamente o pidiéndolo adecuadamente o sugerir que alguien haga algo. Casi siempre sería cuando tienes autoridad "su madre o jefe" o mucha confianza (familia, mejor amigo)

To open up – abrir / abrirse

To tell on – delatar / contar

To tell the truth – decir la verdad

As far as I'm concerned – por lo que a mi concierne

Easier said than done – es más fácil decirlo que hacerlo

For a good cause – por una buena causa

For heaven's sake – por al amor de Dios

For someone's sake – por al amor de alguien *(let's do it for the children's sake – hagámoslo por amor a los niños)*

For nothing – por nada / de gratis

For very little – por muy poco

In my opinion – en mi opinión

To mind your own business – meterte en tus propios asuntos

To raise money – levantar fondos / recolectar dinero *(usualmente para una causa)*

The way I see it – como yo lo veo / de la forma que yo lo veo.

Grammar – Gramática

The auxiliary verb "ought to" – El verbo auxiliar "ought to".

Este verbo auxiliar "ought to – deber" es una forma intermedio entre "should" que es normal y "must" que es más fuerte y con más autoridad. Por lo general solo se usa en afirmativo. "Ought to" expresa ideas tales como deber, necesidad y obligación moral. Normalmente en su forma presente, siempre le seguirá un verbo. Veamos.

We *ought to be* punctual – debemos ser puntuales.

We *ought to help* orphan children – debemos ayudar a los niños huérfanos.

You *ought to visit* your parents once in a while – debes visitar a tus padres de vez en cuando.

Normalmente indica el tiempo presente con acción futura. Puede indicar pasado cuando es seguido por el pasado perfecto infinitivo.

You *ought to have visited* them – debiste haberlos visitado *(era tu responsabilidad, pero no lo hiciste).*

We **ought to have helped** the children – debimos haber ayudar a los niños *(era nuestra responsabilidad, pero no lo hicimos)*

Fíjense bien que "ought to have" está en presente y el siguiente verbo "esta en pasado participio".

Adverbs – Adverbios
Lousy – malísimo / horrible / terrible
Personally - personalmente / por lo que a mi concierne.

Adjectives – Adjetivos
Concerned – preocupado / interesado
Fair – justo *(cuando recibes lo que mereces)*
Honestly – honestamente / realmente

Regular verbs – Verbos regulares
To adopt – adopted – adopted - adoptar
To care – cared – cared – cuidar / atender / preocuparse / importar
To disagree – disagreed – disagreed – disentir / discrepar
To interrupt – interrupted – interrupted – interrumpir
To lie - lied – lied - mentir
To treat – treated – treated – tratar / atender / curar
To trust – trusted – trusted - confiar

Irregular verbs – Verbos irregulares
To beat up – beat up – beaten up – golpear / ganar una pelea *(cuando golpeas a alguien tan fuerte que le haces daño o lastimas. También tiene el sentido de ganar una pelea)*
To swear – swore – sworn – jurar / prometer

The orphanage
Zoe: Hi, Mackenzie, what's new?
Mackenzie: Actually, Dan and I have decided to adopt.
Zoe: Really? Locally?
Mackenzie: No. We thought maybe someone from Latin America or Asia.
Zoe: Easier said than done.
Mackenzie: How's that?
Zoe: Well, first of all, you have to meet the requirements for your state. They'll check your house, and they have all kinds of checks to make sure

you're able to provide a good home. Then you have to meet the requirements of the other country. For instance, China requires adopting parents to be at least thirty years old and to have a certain level of net wealth. Many countries prefer to give the children to someone local. Adoption can be stressful for children, especially when it means changing cultures.

Mackenzie: Wow. Well, the way I see it, we have foster homes and lots of people waiting to adopt here. But in other countries, so many children spend their whole lives in an institution. I've even heard that in some places, the children are kidnapped as soon as they leave the orphanage. If we can help those children to have a better life, I think we ought to do it.

Zoe: It might take a couple years.

Mackenzie: That's okay. It'll give us time to prepare—financially and emotionally. To tell the truth, we've already gone through the initial stages. They told us the orphan will probably need his own bedroom, so we're raising money to add on.

Zoe: Oh, really? How is that coming along?

Mackenzie: Well, I've been making baked goods and crafts to sell. Friends have been donating things, and we've had a few garage sales already. Then there are websites that allow your friends to help you financially. Of course, Dan works overtime when he gets the chance.

Zoe: That's nice. Have most of your friends been supportive of your choice to adopt internationally?

Mackenzie: Yes. Well, there are always some people who disagree. Some people say it's not fair for the adopted child because you'll never love him as much as your own, but I think we will. We know a lot of families who have adopted, and the children seem very happy.

Zoe: I'm sure you'll be an amazing family to some child who really needs one!

Exercises – Ejercicios
Exercise 7.1: Write the verb with "ought to."
Example: You really _ought to eat_ more vegetables. They're so good for your health (eat).

You really _____ your husband. He's killing himself with this new project, and he needs your help (support).

You really _____ someone to teach your son guitar; he's pretty good (find)!
I can't believe you're not participating in the talent show. You have a great voice; you

_____ (sing)!

You know, we _____ our extra room to one of the families that lost their homes in the tornado (offer).

If anyone _____ homeless people, we should; we can make a community pantry where everyone in the area can contribute (help).

Exercise 7.2: Write the letter of the logical response.

But Mom, you didn't tell me you didn't want to me to take the TV apart.

Can you believe they repaired a paved road by pouring dirt over it?

You let your son join the soccer team? What grade did he get in his math class?

How do you get your kids to do their homework?

I went to my first job interview yesterday!

I make them do it. They don't get any privileges— TV, cell phone, going to friends' houses—until they're done.

Really? How did it go?

I don't mean to be rude, Mrs. Smith, but it's really none of your business.

To tell the truth, I'm not surprised. The township saves money in the strangest ways.

Oh, for heaven's sake, couldn't you figure that out on your own?

Conversational Level Three – Nivel de Conversación Tres

Tour across USA

Brenda: What are you doing, Luke?

Luke: I'm planning my trip.

Brenda: What trip?

Luke: I'm going to take a trip to California.

Brenda: Really? How are you going to get there?

Luke: On the bus, of course.

Brenda: You can't be planning to go by bus?

Luke: Why not?

Brenda: You'll go right by the Grand Canyon and miss it! Why don't we all go? There's room in the van for us and our luggage.

Luke: Because you'll turn it into a shopping trip. It'll take us two weeks just to get there, and we won't have any time left to spend in San José.

Brenda: Well, some of us prefer to enjoy the trip than just hurry to get there.

Luke: But that's what my trip is all about—my job interview in San José. I need to see where I can live, too.

Owen: The van needs servicing anyway. It's always reheating and it even shakes!

Cole: Well, if we all **pitch in**, we can get it repaired. We can take turns driving so that we have enough time to enjoy the most important places along the way.

Luke: Well, okay.

Brenda: That sounds good.

Cole: Let's see, there are five of us. I think we could cover the costs with $100 each. Then we'll need another $100 each for gas and tolls. That's if we don't stay in hotels on the way. Everyone pays for their own meals and whatever they want to buy, of course. And we might stay in a suite so we can share the cost of the hotel room in San José.

Owen: Only one suitcase per person, you hear? I'm not going to go all the way across the country with one suitcase under my feet and another one on my lap.

Luke: That's fine by me.

Brenda: Since you were planning to go on the bus anyway.

Luke: Yeah, well, it is my job interview.

Cole: Okay, okay

Luke: When can we leave? Tomorrow? They said I can come anytime I want.

Owen: Are you kidding? It's going to take a week to have the van repaired. And I have to get off work.

Luke: Well, I guess it can wait another week.

Cole: All right. We just have to ask Dad.

Owen: Oh, yeah. Dad.

[Brenda and Luke groan]

Visiting Disneyland

Martina was a hard worker. Her mom worked full

time, so Martina had to learn to take care of herself. One day at school she saw an advertisement online for a free trip to Disneyland. She clicked on the link, but a lot of little windows opened up, so she closed the browser. Martina asked her teacher about it. "I've been thinking about going to Disneyland," she said. "How can I do it?"

Her teacher just stared at her. Martina was not rich; her mother struggled to pay the rent. Their family could probably never go on vacation. But the teacher did not want to hurt her feelings. "You have to work and save up a lot of money—a lot of money. You'd have to buy a plane ticket and tickets to the park, plus you would need money for food and a hotel. You would need a visa, and lots of other things, too."

Martina was not discouraged: "I saw on the Internet that you can win a trip to Disneyland."

"Nothing in life is free, Martina. Be careful of scams. A lot of people make up lies in order to get your information. Be very careful."

"Thank you, Teacher." Martina sat down at her desk, but she did not stop thinking about her dream. She started making plans: she would sell tortillas at first. Then she could save up enough money to sell tamales. Maybe she could even set up a stand to sell food outside the convenience store near her house. Martina had trouble concentrating in class that day.

Martina's mom wasn't very excited about the idea, but she didn't want to discourage her little girl. Martina was surprised at how long it took her to save up a little bit of money. She saved for a few weeks before she was able to make tamales. She worked for several hours and still didn't sell all her tamales. She was so discouraged. She wished she had a storefront, so that she could make money faster. The convenience store manager felt bad for Martina and let her sell outside his business, but he knew she would never make enough to go to Disneyland. He told her she could leave her tamales inside the store, and he would sell them for her. Soon, she had tamales in stores all over town. She started to make more money. She opened a bank account to store her savings. It took two years, but Martina made it. She was able to take her mom to Disneyland! And when she came back, she went back to her tamale business and saved up money for college!

Republicans and Democrats

Matt: Hey, Dad, I went to register to vote, but they asked what party I wanted to vote for in the primaries.

Dad: Yes. That's the policy in our state.

Matt: But what party should I choose?

Dad: You have to decide that, Matt.

Matt: But Dad, I don't understand which party is better. Your family is kind of grass-roots conservative, but you're a democrat, and mom is from a more liberal, change-the-world background, and she's a republican.

Dad: Yes, that is kind of ironic. We usually think of the republican party as conserving traditional values and keeping the government from limiting individual rights, whereas the democratic party is more often associated with big government and help for minorities, trying to change society. But you shouldn't join a party just because your mom or I did. You need to make your own decision. And you don't have to vote for the party you join. Neither of them is perfect. In fact, we both vote for people from both parties.

Matt: What about the other parties?

Dad: Oh, I don't know. They never seem to have much of a chance to win, and so we don't usually vote for them. People say a vote for a third-party candidate is a vote wasted. But you ought to research all the candidates and decide who you agree with most. Then, whoever you choose, you can register for that party and vote for him or her in the primaries.

Matt: I don't think I really agree with any of them completely.

Dad: I understand. It's hard to know what politicians really believe anyway. A lot of people end up voting for the person they consider to be the lesser of two evils.

Matt: Who do you think will win?

Dad: I wish I knew. If I knew that, I'd be a very rich man. Let's do this. Go do some more research. Write down each party and the candidates for that party. Then write the pros and cons of each candidate, and come back and tell me who you agree with most. Then you can either register for that party and vote in the primaries, or wait and vote in the general election.

Matt: Okay, Dad.

College system in US

There are five main stages to school in the US. These are preschool/kindergarten, elementary school, junior high, high school, and college (university level). The requirements for each level are mainly determined by the state. Each state publishes requirements for certifying teachers and standards that the teachers have to cover in class and include in their portfolios. The state also determines requirements for people who want to educate their children at home. Often, home schoolers have to take a portfolio to an authorized evaluator so that they can continue home schooling the next school year.

States decide at what age schooling becomes compulsory. A few states require children to begin schooling at age five, many more at age six. Pennsylvania and Washington allow children to begin as late as age eight! In preschool, children can learn numbers, shapes, patterns, and alphabet sounds. In kindergarten, they study **phonics** so that they can learn to read. English spelling is no longer closely related to pronunciation ever since French was spoken in England for over three centuries. So now, English-speaking children must study rules of spelling, learning how to pronounce particular vowel and consonant combinations in "word families."

In elementary school, grades one to six, children

learn how to learn. They learn the basics of math, English (reading comprehension and writing), science, and history/geography/social studies.

In junior high, seventh to ninth grade, the standard is raised a bit higher. Students become more autonomous, with regular homework assignments and tests that require more memorization and independent study. Junior high is also called middle school.

The next step is high school, grades ten to twelve. If students want to go to college, they have to make sure they are in the college preparatory track in high school. Some high schools use terms such as the basic, advanced, and honors tracks to distinguish those students who are completing studies in order to immediately join the work force (basic), those who want to go to college (advanced), and those who want to test out of some college courses (honors) so that they can earn their college degree earlier.

Technically, there are several colleges in a university, but most people call university "college." In a liberal arts college, students take more general courses in the first two years, and courses specific to their major in the last two years. Underclassmen are called freshmen the first year, sophomores the second year. Upperclassmen are juniors their third year and seniors their final year. Universities have a special system for showing students' grade point averages based on the letter (A-B-C-D-F) and the number of credits earned. A good average will earn cum laude upon graduation. An excellent average earns magna cum laude, and a nearly perfect average earns suma cum laude.

University System in US

Today's **job market** requires a college-level education in order to maintain a **decent standard of living**. However, college is expensive! Community colleges offer significant discounts for local students, but what if you want to study humanities, and the local schools offer only science and law majors? There are huge books and entire websites dedicated to describing fellowships, loans, and scholarships available for students. Most of them are available to students in a particular field, **e.g.**, law, science education, foreign languages. Fellowships require the student to do something in exchange for the money; for instance, a science student might be asked to do research. Loans, of course, must be repaid. Scholarships are sometimes offered to anyone studying a particular major, to people within a particular minority group (e.g., women, Hispanics), to students with an outstanding GPA (Grade Point Average) in high school, or to the student who writes the best essay on a particular subject.

There are many opportunities for international students in the US, with scholarships offered exclusively for them nationwide and at many colleges. In fact, most colleges will probably have discounts (**i.e.**, small scholarships) for international students and minority groups. Once you arrive, you will probably have to maintain a particular GPA in order to keep the scholarship, but a good GPA can also help you to earn additional scholarships. Some organizations and colleges may offer a full scholarship (100% of tuition and possibly also housing/food) for students who they think may make the world a better place.

In any case, make sure you can prove that you can pay for your schooling before you enter the country. Talk with the school you plan to attend to get help securing your student visa. If you plan to get a work scholarship or to get a job on the side, discuss these plans with your admissions counselor. There are limitations on working under a student visa. Make sure that you can have your high school transcripts sent to the school and that they will be accepted. Some schools also require a certain level of English-speaking ability for admittance. Others will admit students with lower English ability but require them to take extra courses in English (at the normal cost of college tuition).

American music

The United States owes much of its musical heritage to the African-American slaves. Slaves had to work long hours in the fields, and they were not allowed to speak their native languages or complain about their situation. So when slave owners encouraged them to go to church, they were glad to have the opportunity to socialize and talk a little bit more freely. Inspired by hymns of the Great

Awakening, African-Americans made up songs to sing at church and in the fields. It's not hard to imagine why the slaves identified with the Jews: "When Israel was in Egypt's land, Let my people go; Oppressed so hard they could not stand, Let My people go."

Negro spirituals give encouragement to endure the difficulties of slave life, and they give hope of freedom. These messages were veiled in biblical allusions, so that slave owners would not prohibit them from singing these songs that gave them hope of one day being free.

Since slaves were not allowed to learn to read, they had to sing the songs from memory. Usually one person would sing a line, and the others would repeat it. Some of the spirituals, such as "Swing Low, Sweet Chariot" and "The Gospel Train," may have hidden meanings referring to the Underground Railroad, a route to Canada for escaping slaves. "Canaan" may refer to Canada, "home" might be freedom. These songs definitely encouraged slaves with the possibility of deliverance. Most of these songs are still popular. If you ever feel like quitting, you can sing the "Gospel Plow," which alludes to Luke 9:62 in the lyrics "keep your hand on the plow." Don't give up!

These songs gave back to the genre that inspired them; the genre of negro spirituals inspired gospel songs such as "Just a Closer Walk With Thee." Jazz, which is now popular all over the world, was also developed by, and usually interpreted by, African-Americans such as Louis Armstrong. This music uses

European instruments and harmony, but definitely has African rhythm and style.

Another distinctly American genre is bluegrass, which originated in the Appalachian region. This music became extremely popular when recordings were made in Bristol, Tennessee. And these recordings led to the development of another popular American genre—country music.

Level Three Tests – Examenes del Nivel Tres

Estos son los exámenes para pasar el nivel tres. Asegúrense de tomar su tiempo y completarlos correctamente. Una vez los hayan completado y estén completamente seguros que han terminado. Pueden presentarlos a un amigo de habla inglesa para que los revise y les diga si lo hicieron bien, o pueden enviarme un email con sus exámenes. Sin en algún punto, aun están dudosos, deberán repasarlo y asegurarse de dominarlo muy bien. El tercer nivel es esencial para todo el aprendizaje, sin dominarlo bien, no podremos aprender bien. Es imperativo dominar a la perfección cada uno de los conceptos presentados en este nivel. ***Good luck once again!***

Test: Units 1-3

Test 1.1: Underline the correct form of the verb.

When she heard the news, her eyes **fill/filled/filling** with tears.

She was **hold/held/holding** the ruby when the detective arrived.

You can't play games with me! This **means/meant/meaning** war!

That poor girl looks like she is **runs away/ran away/running away** from home.

Why does she need a new coat? Has she **wears out/wore out/worn out/wearing out** the old one already?

The slave **hides/hid/hidden/hiding** above the barn until they stopped looking for her.

You have to **tear/tore/torn/tearing** the pages out and put them in a **three-ring binder**.

There isn't any ice. The ice cubes haven't **freeze/froze/frozen/freezing** yet.

Oh, no! He **throws away/threw away/thrown away/throwing away** all of the bank records!

I really enjoy **teach/taught/teaching**!

Test 1.2: Underline the correct word or group of words.

My grandparents are visiting. They **may/maybe** stay for a month!

Mom likes chocolate. Dad likes strawberry. I like mint **herself/ourselves/myself**.

I **can/could/was able to** finish the report last night!

There used to **is/are/was/be** an Italian restaurant on this street.

My mom has trouble **get/got/gotten/getting** to sleep.

You can watch **wherever/whenever/whatever** you want. Just don't turn on the TV.

Whoever/wherever/whatever ate the ice cream, you had better buy some more!

We bought ice cream and cake, but the birthday girl didn't like **one/both/either** of them.

If it rains, you **are going to get/will get/got** wet.

Mom asked **if you want/do you want** to come to our house.

Test 1.3: Write the letter to complete the sentence.

_____ If you don't eat your vegetables

_____ He must be sick;

_____ I can't decide which purse to buy;

_____ If we don't go now,

_____ We can't be out of sugar;

A. we'll never make it to their house before dinner time.
B. I want all of them!
C. you'll probably get sick.
D. I just bought a two-pound bag yesterday!
E. he would never say no to pecan pie if he felt okay.

Test 2: Units 4-7
Test 2.1: Correct the error in each sentence. There is one grammatical error in each sentence.
What have you been do lately?
Look at that man dancing in the rain! He must is crazy.
If I had more money, I help you.
I wish I have a bigger house.
You really ought to bought more fruit.
Test 2.2: Underline the correct form.
You **can't be / must be** serious! I just saw her last

week, and she was fine! How can she be dying?

The store **can't be / must be** closed. Look there's only one light on, and I don't see anyone inside.

He **can't be / must be** the thief. I know him. He's a very nice guy, very honest too.

She **can't be / must be** hungry. It's been five hours since she had lunch.

They **can't be / must be** angry. He was so rude to them!

Test 2.3: Complete the sentence: Underline the correct form.

This is how to make fettuccine alfredo: First, the pasta **has been boiling / is boiled.** . . .

The bread **has been taking / is taken** from the oven every morning at 7:00.

We **have been opening / is opened** the store early ever since Easter.

Clocks **have been turning back / will be turned back** next week.

The supervisor **has been asking / is asked** for a raise. What should we do?

Test 3.1: Underline the logical word/phrase.

If you're going to Niagara Falls, you have to take your passport. **Likewise / Otherwise**, they won't let you back into the United States.

When Amy thought she might get scarlet fever, she decided **to leave her dad alone / to leave her pictures to her dad.**

Are you watching soap operas? I **can't stand / can't wait** them!

I forgot my homework. And **to make matters worse / that's nothing new**, I didn't study for the test.

My aunt says it's bad **to tell someone's fortune / to tell the truth.**

Don't worry about losing the lottery. Maybe it's **the way I see it / for the best.** You won't have to worry about people asking you for money all the time.

Well, it's been nice seeing you. **Help yourself! / Take care!**

So you're Trixie? It's nice to finally meet you in person. **Keep in touch! / Welcome aboard!** You are going to love it here!

Good luck / Good gracious, I left the dog in the car!

I can't believe it. It looks like my dream of going to college is finally **coming true / getting to the point.**

This phone is **good gracious / good for nothing**. It won't even turn on anymore!

Please **have a seat / pay attention**. The doctor will see you in a few minutes.

That's a lot of money to pay for a balloon, but I guess it's **for a good cause / for nothing.**

If I were you / The way I see it, I would just calm down and wait to see what the doctor says.

Someone stole my wallet, but **it depends / thank goodness,** I ran into Uncle Joe, and he gave me a ride.

Now and then! / What do you say? Can we get a cat?

No, I'm not offended that you called me old. **After all / Day after day,** no one will ever believe that I'm older than you.

Son, it's very important not **to tell the truth / to tell on your classmates.** You won't have any friends!

Shut up! / Darn! That's not how you should talk to your grandpa!

Hurry up! It's time to go. **Come true / Come on,** let's go.

Test 3.2: Write the correct form for the first or second conditional.

If they had a dog, a burglar **won't / wouldn't** be able to break into their house.

If I raise enough money, I **will / would** go to Ireland.

If you were my dad, you **won't / wouldn't** talk to me that way.

If I had a car, I **will / could** get a better job.

If we leave now, we **will / would** have time to stop at a restaurant.

Test 3.3: Underline the correct form of the verb.

Metamorphosis was writing/written by Franz Kafka.

I've been waiting/waited for fifteen minutes.

Watergate salad is making/made with pistachio pudding, pineapple, nuts, and whipped topping.

Garbage used to be burning/burnt in people's back yards.

Mark has been studying / studied for a very difficult test.

Verb list – Lista de verbos
To adopt – adoptar
To agree (with) – acordar

To allow – permitir / autorizar / dejar

To appear – aparecer / parecer

To arrange – organizar / arreglar

To arrest – arrestar

To ask for – preguntar por / pedir

To bake – hornear

To be able - ser capaz

To beat up – golpear / ganar una pelea

To belong – pertenecer

To blow up - explotar

To break down - dañarse

To build – construir

To burn – quemar

To camp – acampar

To care – cuidar / atender / preocuparse / importar

To check – chequear / verificar

To cheer – animar / alentar

To chuckle – reírse entre los dientes

To collect – cobrar / recolectar

To cure – curar

To decide - decidir

To deserve – merecer

To design - diseñar

To develop - desarrollar

To disagree - disentir / discrepar

To disappear – desaparecer

To discuss – discutir

To divorce - divorciarse

To dream – soñar

To dress up – vestirse / disfrazarse

To drop – caer / dejar caer

To drown – ahogarse
To elect – elegir
To empty – vaciar
To encourage – animar / alentar / estimular
To equip (for / with) – equipar (para / con)
To explain – explicar
To export – exportar
To fall down – caerse
To feed – alimentar
To fill – llenar
To fire – disparar
To freeze – congelar
To go on – continuar / avanzar / seguir
To grow – crecer
To hide – esconder
To hijack – secuestrar
To hire – contratar / emplear
To import – importar
To inform – informar
To interrupt – interrumpir
To interview - entrevistar
To invent – inventar / crear
To invest – invertir
To knock on - tocar
To laugh – reír
To launch – lanzar / inaugurar
To let – dejar / permitir
To light – encender / iluminar
To manage – organizar / lograr / administrar
To manufacture – fabricar / manufacturar
To marry - casarse

To mean – significar / querer decir

To mess up – desordenar / estropear / arruinar / ensuciar

To milk – ordeñar

To move – mover

To mow – podar

To notice – notar / percibir

To offer – ofrecer

To organize – organizar

To own – poseer

To paint – - pintar

To park – parquear / estacionar

To pedal – pedalear

To plant – plantar / sembrar

To pray – orar

To predict – predecir

To produce – producir

To protect (from) – proteger (de)

To pull – halar

To push – empujar

To put away – guardar / retirar

To raise – criar / levantar

To realize – darse cuenta / entender

To redecorate – redecorar

To reduce – reducir

To reelect – reelegir

To return – regresar

To roast - asar

To run away - run away - huir

To sail – navegar

To save – salvar / guardar

Nivel Tres

To score - anotar
To seem - parecer
To serve – servir
To service – dar servicio o mantenimiento a un aparato
To settle down – establecerse / resolver / sentar cabeza
To shake – agitar / sacudir
To shoot – disparar / tirar / arrojar
To shop – comprar (en tiendas)
To smile – sonreír
To snore – roncar
To solve - resolver
To sound - sonar
To spend – gastar
To stop – detener
To straighten up – enderezar / ordenar
To suggest – sugerir
To suppose – suponer
To surf – surfear
To swear – jurar / prometer
To teach – enseñar
To tear – rasgar
To test – probar / examinar
To throw away – botar / arrojar / desechar
To touch – tocar / palpar
To train – entrenar
To treat – tratar / atender / curar
To trouble – molestar / preocupar
To trust – confiar
To try on – probarse (ropa)

To vote – votar

To wear out – gastar / desgastar

To welcome – dar la bienvenida

To wind up – dar cuerda

To wish (for / that) – desear (por / que)

To wonder – preguntarse / asombrarse / maravillarse

Grammar Summary

Lesson 1

Pronouns and adverbs – Pronombres y adverbios
Reflexive – Emphatic pronouns – Pronombres reflexivos y enfáticos.
Pronoun + of – Pronombre más of
Adjectives – Adjetivos
Regular verbs – Verbos regulares
Irregular verbs – Verbos irregulares

Lesson 2

Forms of "Can" and "To be able to" – Formas de "Can" y "To be able to".
Forms of "must" and "have to" – Formas de "must" y "have to".
The Adverb "Back" – El adverbio "back".
Indirect Commands – Órdenes indirectos.
Reported Speech – Discurso indirecto
Conditional (type 1) – Condicional (tipo 1).
Conjunctions – Conjunciones.
Adjectives – Adjetivos
Regular verbs – Verbos regulares
Irregular verbs – Verbos irregulares

Lesson 3

The auxiliary "May" and "Maybe" – El auxiliar "May" y "Maybe".

143

"There is / are" with auxiliary verbs – "There is / are" con verbos auxiliares.

Verbs plus "ing" form – Verbos más la forma "ing".

Reported Speech in Present and Past – Discurso indirecto en presente y pasado.

Reported questions "ask" – Preguntas discurso indirecto "ask".

Adverbs – Adverbios

Adjectives – Adjetivos

Regular verbos – Verbos regulares

Irregular verbs – Verbos irregulares

Lesson 4

Present perfect progressive – Presente perfecto continuo.

Using "can't be" and "must be" – Usando "can't be" y "must be".

The word "As" – La palabra "As"

Verbs of Sense and Perception – Verbos de sentidos y percepción.

The passive voice – La voz pasiva

The impersonal "you" – El "you" impersonal.

Adjectives – Adjetivos

Regular verbs – Verbos regulares

Irregular verbs – Verbos irregulares

Lesson 5

Conditional type 2 – Condicional tipo 2.

Some uses of "would" – Algunos usos de "would".

The verb "to wish" – El verbo "to wish".

The passive voice – La voz pasiva

Nouns formed from verbs – Nombres formados de verbos.

Adverbs – Adverbios
Adjectives – Adjetivos
Regular verbs – Verbos regulares
Irregular verbs – Verbos irregulares

Lesson 6
To have + noun + past participle – To have + sustantivo + pasado participio.
To need + ing – To need + ing
Agreeing and disagreeing – Acuerdos y desacuerdos.
Conjunction "so that" – Conjunción "so that"
Adverbs – Adverbios
Adjectives – Adjetivos
Regular verbs – Verbos regulares
Irregular verbs – Verbos irregulares

Lesson 7
The auxiliary verb "ought to" – El verbo auxiliar "ought to".
Adverbs – Adverbios
Adjectives – Adjetivos
Regular verbs – Verbos regulares
Irregular verbs – Verbos irregulares

Answers to exercises – Respuestas de los ejercicios

Como terminaron sus exámenes y se aseguraron de dominar cada concepto, pueden verificar las respuestas al final del libro. Me he tomado la libertad de ofrecerles las respuestas de todos los ejercicios de cada lección asi también como los del examen de nivel. Pero no hagan trampa, solo ustedes pierden si hacen trampa. *See you on the fourth volume.*

Lesson 1
Answers to Exercise 1.1:
myself
themselves
ourselves
itself
yourself
Answers to Exercise 1.2
whenever
Wherever
Whatever
whoever
whatever
Answers to Exercise 1.3:
b
d
a
e

c

Answers to Exercise 1.4:
by the way
Help yourself
Take care
You're kidding
come on

Lesson 2
Answers to Exercise 2.1:
can
cannot/can't
was able to
could
not been able to
can
could
not be able to

Answers to Exercise 2.2:
A/P
A
A
A/P
A
A
A
A
P
P

Answers to Exercise 2.3:
need
brought
walk back
gave
give
coming back
take
drove
want
ran back

Answers to Exercise 2.4:
The policeman says (that) you win a bicycle if you collect four of these (those) tickets.

The teacher says to bring pictures to class tomorrow.

Uncle Jerry says (that) you catch more flies with honey.

The veterinarian says (that) the best thing is to wash him (the dog).

The mechanic says (that) the car will be as good as new.

Answers to Exercise 2.5:
will get/gets
will take/can take
make
will kill
won't have

Lesson 3
Answers to Exercise 3.1:
Mark said he loved her.

They said this/that town was beautiful.

He asked where he/she was.

Her parents promised that they would not throw away her toys. / Her parents promised that they were not going to throw away her toys.

He told his daughter to go to sleep.

The player said he scored more points than any other player.

John said there might be mice down here/there.

The policeman said he found that hard to believe.

The principal asked if she was sure her husband would come.

Mac reported that Tom stopped to help a lady cross the street.

Answers to Exercise 3.2:
be

eating

drinking

travel

hiring

to rain/raining

watching/to watch

to pay/paying

to finish

to visit

Answers to Exercise 3.3:
sweetly
nice
neat
nervously
definitely

Lesson 4
Answers to Exercise 4.1:
can't be
must be
seems like
can't be
must be
must be
must be
can't be
seemed like
seems like

Answers to Exercise 4.2:
has been designing
've been training
hasn't been producing
's been shaking
have been raising
've been wondering
've been painting
have been appearing
've been parking
've been saving

Answers to Exercise 4.3:
is grown
will be kept
is made
was filmed
be produced
have been reported

Lesson 5
Answers to Exercise 5.1:
was . . . encouraged
was reelected
were planted
has been organized
was invested

Answers to Exercise 5.2:
past intention
typical
wish
typical
used to
wish
used to
past intention
used to
wish

Answers to Exercise 5.3:
had; would buy

were; would tell
tried; would recognize
wore; wouldn't be
agreed; would cry

Lesson 6
Answers to Exercise 6.1:
c
b
a
e
d

Answers to Exercise 6.2:
Her hair needs trimming; she's going to have her hair trimmed.

My shoes need repairing; I want to have them [my shoes] repaired.

Our tires need replacing; we want to have them [our tires] replaced.

Their corn needs harvesting; they plan to have it harvested.

George's shirts need [dry] cleaning; he plans to have them dry cleaned.

Suggested answers to Exercise 6.3: Answers will vary.
Of course she wouldn't; Of course not
I am absolutely positive she did
I definitely was
not; I guess it might; I guess it could

they can; they might be able to
you're probably right; that's probably true

Lesson 7

Answers to Exercise 7.1:
ought to support
ought to find
ought to sing
ought to offer
ought to help

Answers to Exercise 7.2:
e
d
c
a
b

Answers to Level Three Tests – Respuesta de los Examenes del Nivel Tres

Answers to Test 1.1:
filled
holding
means
running away
worn out
hid
tear
frozen
threw away
teaching
Answers to Test 1.2:
may
myself
was able to
be
getting
whatever
Whoever
either
will get
if you want
Answers to Test 1.3:
c

e
b
a
d

Answers to Test 2.1:
have you been do → have you been doing
must is crazy → must be crazy
I help → I would help
I wish I have → I wish I had
ought to bought → ought to buy / ought to have bought

Answers to Test 2.2:
can't be
must be
can't be
must be
must be

Answers to Test 2.3:
is boiled
is taken
have been opening
will be turned back
has been asking

Answers to Test 3.1:
Otherwise
to leave her pictures to her dad
can't stand
to make matters worse
to tell someone's fortune
for the best
Take care!

Welcome aboard!
Good gracious
coming true
good for nothing
have a seat
for a good cause
If I were you
thank goodness
What do you say?
After all
to tell on your classmates
Shut up!
Come on

Answers to Test 3.2:
wouldn't
will
wouldn't
could
will

Answers to Test 3.3:
written
waiting
made
burnt
studying

Conclusión

Muchas gracias por seleccionar el *Curso Completo de Inglés – Nivel Tres* por Yeral E. Ogando para su aprendizaje. Por fin, han llegado al final del tercer nivel, por lo tanto, ya pueden hablar inglés fluido y están listos para el nivel cuatro.

Les exhorto que continúen practicando y hablando inglés en todo momento, ya les he dicho que la Practica hace al Maestro. Visiten mi pagina de internet para más información.

God bless you and see you in volumen three.

Dr. Yeral E. Ogando
www.aprendeis.com

BONO GRATIS

Estimado Estudiante,

Necesitas descargar el audio MP3 para usar este increíble método para aprender inglés. Visita este link:
http://aprendeis.com/ingles-audio-nivel3/
Usuario "ennivel3"
Contraseña "en32016"

Solo tienes que descargar el archivo comprimido, descomprimirlo y estas listo para iniciar tu experiencia al mundo del inglés.

Si quieres compartir tu experiencia, comentario o possible sugerencia, siempre podrás contactarme a info@aprendeis.com

Muchas gracias por estudiar el *Curso Completo de Inglés – Nivel Tres* y por escuchar mis instrucciones.

Caros afectos,
Dr. Yeral E. Ogando

Otros libros escritos por Yeral E. Ogando

Conciencia: El Héroe Dentro de Ti

Curso Completo de Inglés – Nivel Uno
Curso Completo de Inglés – Nivel Dos

Yeral E. Ogando Proviene de un origen muy humilde y continúa siendo un humilde siervo de nuestro Señor Todopoderoso; entendiendo que no somos más que recipientes y el Señor nos llama y nos envía también a hacer Su trabajo, no nuestro trabajo. Lucas 17:10 "Así también vosotros, cuando hayáis hecho todo lo que os ha sido ordenado, decid: Siervos inútiles somos, pues lo que debíamos hacer, hicimos".

El Señor Ogando nació en el Caribe, República Dominicana. Es el padre amado de dos bellas chicas

Yeiris y Tiffany.

Jesús le trajo a Sus pies en la edad de 16-17 años. Desde entonces, ha servido como Co-pastor, Pastor, profesor de la Biblia en las escuelas, consejero de jóvenes, plantador y fundador de iglesias. Actualmente está sirviendo como Secretario para la Iglesia Reformada Dominicana así como de enlace para Haití y EE.UU.

Fluido en varias lenguas el Señor Ogando es el Creador y dueño de un Ministerio de Traducción Online que opera desde el 2007; con traductores cristianos Nativos en más de 25 países. (www.christian-translation.com),

Lo más apasionante acerca de su Ministerio de Traducción es que miles de personas están recibiendo la Palabra de Dios en su lengua nativa diariamente y cientos de ministerios logran llegar al mundo a través del trabajo de Christian-translation.com junto con su red de traducción de 17 sitios web relacionados con traducciones cristianas, a diferentes lenguas.